D1551475

A BOOK OF PRIVATE PRAYER

For the Garveys and Hogans

A BOOK OF
PRIVATE PRAYER

by

Dom Hubert van Zeller

TEMPLEGATE
Publishers

SPRINGFIELD, ILLINOIS

III

Nihil obstat: A. M. Young, O.S.B. August 5, 1958

Imprimatur: H. K. Byrne, O.S.B. Abbot President
August 11, 1958

IV

PREFACE

The arrangement of this book is best accounted for by indicating the two kinds of reader here envisaged. The one comes to it for material which he can turn into his own form of prayer; the other for a written text which he can take as it stands and recite before God. The book is accordingly divided into two sections, the earlier providing mostly subject-matter and the later providing the formula and the frame. This explains the difference in length between what is proposed for consideration and what for recitation or repetition. The prayers that we actually *say,* as distinct from those that arise out of what we *think,* will call for a more compact expression. In suggesting thoughts (which can then be translated either into words of our own or into further thoughts) the text can afford to be fuller. But the above division is very loose. There will be prayers in the prayer-idiom among the earlier devotions, and ideas for personal elaboration will be found among the later. Indeed the whole point about any book of this sort is that it tries to furnish the soul not with a rigid letter of prayer but with an impulse to pray. It is with this in view—directing the soul towards interior articulation, individual and not stereotyped—that these verbal compositions are submitted.

Contents

Part 1 Considerations

VII

Part 2 Occasional Prayers

Part 1

Considerations

I ADDRESS MY PRAYERS, today and every day, to the
holy Trinity. Not only my prayers but also my work,
pleasures, decisions, difficulties
✠ MORNING and sufferings are directed to
the glory of the Father, Son,
and Holy Spirit. If I am faithful to this idea, returning to it and making it actual as the occasions
follow one another during the course of the day, I
shall come by God's grace to the habit of recollection. My work, pleasures, decisions, difficulties and
sufferings will themselves be acts of prayer.

Father, into your hands I commend the hours
which will be spent between now and the time
when I come again in the evening to praise your
name. If chances occur during the day of renewing
my purpose and recollecting my soul I ask to be
reminded of my present intention. Since it is from
you that I have received my life, it is to you that I
want to refer every moment of it. If human fathers
can be counted upon to interest themselves in the
affairs of their children, I know that you must care
far more about how I spend my day. Father, this
day belongs to you: arrange it as you will, and let
me not disappoint you during it.

To Jesus Christ I look for example and criteria
of action. May you be with me throughout the day,
Lord, to show me how you would have acted had
the circumstances of my life been yours. May your
influence come to be even more immediate, so that
I can trace your action within the activities which I

2

call my own. If I am truly a member of your body, and if the doctrine of your indwelling means that I possess you in my mind and heart, then the acts that I do can come to be performed as acts of yours. I act now not I, but you act in me and through me and for me. May the evidence of this appear today in the prayerfulness and charity with which I meet the changing situation from hour to hour. Allow your sacred mind to reflect itself and express itself in mine.

To you, Holy Spirit, I look especially for the light which will let me see beyond the material purpose to the spiritual. All day long I shall be placed in physical contact with physical things; grant that I may understand the physical order in its supernatural context. Moving among human beings, addressing myself to temporal concerns, finding the natural everywhere I look, I have great need of the insight which can come only from you. May your grace enable me to handle earthly things in relation to heavenly, temporal things in terms of eternity. Left to myself I see only the external, the superficial, the unreal. Given your light I shall come to look below the surface, seeing there the reflection of your truth.

Holy Trinity, one God, receive and bless the issues of today. So far as I am given to foresee them, certain events can be expected to take place in it. For these I must prepare myself, as I am trying now to do. But it is the unexpected that is

3

likely, unless you give me your help, to cause the trouble. If I should be faced with sudden disappointments, sudden temptations, sudden interruptions, I shall need more than mere natural presence of mind; I shall need the supernatural point of view. I shall need patience, trust, and charity.

In addition to this morning dedication, I lay before you the needs of others during this coming day: the needs of my family and friends, of the sick, of the dying, of sinners, of unbelievers, and of the dead. May all receive the graces which, were I in their conditions, I would wish to receive myself.

I COME NOW before the Holy Trinity with a twofold purpose: first to account for how the day has been spent, and second to ask

✠ EVENING for protection and blessing for the night. Such is the immediate purpose, and the form which my prayer will take; the overall purpose of my evening devotions is of course—as the purpose of every prayer-act must be—to give glory to God. In reporting on the conduct of the day I am not merely finding an excuse for talking about myself; in asking to be spared the dangers of the night I am not merely ensuring a good night's rest. God, and not myself, should be the object of my interest. I pray in order to praise.

Father, to you do I present the balance-sheet of

my day. Like the awkward and difficult son that I am, I stand in your presence confused at the evidence of my inadequacy, ungenerosity, failure. Having started off in the morning on the impulse of your grace, I soon lost sight of the standard proposed. If I examine myself now on how far I really tried to maintain a spirit of recollection, how far I tried to make filial love and not servile fear the motive of whatever good I did or whatever evil I avoided, I must have much of which to accuse myself. But like a guilty and neglectful son before a human father, I come with absolute confidence to ask your pardon.

In the same way I can examine my conscience in the light of Christ's example and the terms of this morning's dedication. Have I looked for your reflection, Lord, in the people whom I have met in the course of the day? Have I approached the problems that have been presented to me as though you were approaching them through me? Have I tried to let your patience, humility, tolerance and love radiate out to others? Or have I done things hurriedly, arrogantly, without thought for the feelings of others, trusting in my own ability to carry them through? However badly I have reproduced your outlook today, tomorrow let me have the grace of following your lead more closely.

Perhaps my mistake has been to think of the Holy Spirit only as wisdom and not enough as love. Perhaps I have expected you to light up my path through the day, making everything clear and smooth, instead of simply relying upon you to increase my generosity. If my heart were to respond more immediately to your grace, I would not mind being left in the dark and having to stumble over the rough ground. But because I am slow to love, I am quick to lose confidence. I pray that your wisdom may teach me not only what to do but also how to go on when there seems to be nothing that I can do. On those occasions when my human judgment is in abeyance, when my prayers for light seem only to bring further darkness, I pray that I may take my stand on love alone. Love means sacrifice, and I must learn to do without the consolation of knowing what to do next. Even if I am to do without consolation of any sort, whether in my decisions or my hopes or my securities, I know that your grace will make such a situation somehow supportable. For whatever graces I have received today, Lord, I thank you.

Turning from the day to the night, I ask to be kept from harm in soul and body during the hours which lie between now and when I wake to praise your name in the morning. Keep me alert against temptation, and if I am unable to sleep let me remember to turn to you in prayer. Asleep or awake, I want to leave myself in your presence. I pray for those who are to die tonight, also for the suffering, the tempted, and the fallen.

WHEN I AM PRESENT AT MASS I am present at the prayer of Christ addressed to God the Father. If

☩ THE MASS

the Mass means all to me that it should, I am not only present *at* but present *in* the the prayer of Christ addressed to God the Father. To hear Mass must suggest something more to me than merely listening to the sound of its words. Just as I can follow the points of a debate without taking part in the discussion so I can follow the words and ceremonies of the Mass without taking part in it. By hearing Mass, in the literal sense, I can satisfy my obligation; it is by taking part in the Mass that I fulfill its implication.

If the Mass is no more to me than a concentration of sacred symbols in the presence of which I pay my debt of homage to God, I might equally well stay at home and devise a liturgy of my own to be performed before relics, statues and blessed candles. But because the Mass is the concentration of Christ's life, doctrine, prayer and death, I come before the altar and unite my prayer-activity with His. The reason why the Church requires of us attendance at Mass is not that at least half an hour of our prayer is guaranteed—this could have been secured by making any other religious exercise obligatory — but that for at least half an hour Christ's prayer is ours for the asking.

Every time I hear the words *Dominus vobiscum,* and I hear them nine times in the course of the

7

Mass, I am reminded that Christ's prayer is mine and that mine is His. From the opening psalm till the last gospel the same idea is stressed. I find it in the sequence of the liturgical seasons, in the doctrine of the Eucharist, in the history of the early Church, in the contemporary revival of liturgical thought and practice. In spite of this I frequently catch myself out in putting more store by my own devotions than by the infinite merits of the Mass's prayer.

I pray that while my senses follow the words and movements of the Mass my soul may follow its meaning and its summons. I pray that my whole being may be so steeped in the significance of Christ's sacrifice as to correspond instinctively: I too must surrender completely to the Father's will, I too must submit to being treated by human beings in whatever way they choose. What else but this do I mean when I place myself in spirit with the host on the paten, when I ask to be included in the offering of the chalice? Jesus Christ, *qui humanitatis nostrae fieri dignatus est particeps* as we read in the missal at the moment when the wine and the water mingle in the chalice, catches up into his own oblation of himself the acts of self-giving which are made by us. The prayer goes on to ask that we may be made partakers of His divinity, *ejus divinitatis esse consortes.*

Lord, together with the offering of bread and wine I offer the needs of the whole world, the intentions of those whom I love and of those who have asked me to mention their needs in my prayers. I join in spirit with the prayers of Mary and the saints, with the everlasting chorus of the blessed who sing their *Sanctus* before you. Of the four ends of the Mass let me be sure to give first place to that of praise. Your glory is the primary purpose, and when I have done my best to pay homage to your name, which I do here and now in this present sacrifice which invites my participation, then let me know how best to ask pardon, express thanks, and frame the petitions which you want to hear. Lord, take my Mass prayers and shape them as you will.

WE ARE GIVEN THE THEME for our eucharistic devotions in the *Domine, non sum dignus* of the Mass. Any other preparation before it, any other thanksgiving after it, than that of humble confidence in the power of grace to make good what is wanting to our own response, would be unworthy and wasted. The grace of holy communion is so infinitely beyond what we deserve, that to think of receiving it adequately by any industry of ours is sheer presumption. All that we can do is to dispose ourselves—*ad te levavi animam meam*—and even in this we are relying upon the action of grace. Lord, dispose me, prepare me, unite yourself to me, and manage my thanksgiving for me. My whole care is cast upon you, for I know

✠ HOLY COMMUNION

that you have care of me. Knowing that it is your action that conditions my reaction, I pray that your action may be such as call out from me whatever good it is that you yourself have placed there.

The more I am able to see into the meaning of the divine indwelling the more am I likely to benefit by my communions. Though I can never expect to fathom its full implication, I can at least remind myself of your abiding presence in my soul. In coming to me sacramentally you are coming to your own—to what your grace is making increasingly your own—and my whole desire is to give you, in addition to perfect freedom af access, permanent habitation. Grant that as the distractions of the day crowd in upon me when I finish my thanksgiving in the church, I may keep up the continuity by returning to the thought of your visit in the morning. If my communion is at an evening Mass, let me be reminded of its grace during the night and when I wake. In this way my union with you will not be a matter of moments merely, but a matter of relationship. Sanctifying grace is a matter of relationship; religion is a matter of relationship; the theological virtues are a matter of relationship. But though I know all this, I know also that the relationship is only intermittently appreciated. I pray that my communions may make me more habitually aware of your indwelling in my soul.

In this present communion I pray not only for my own personal needs but for those of all mankind: for the conversion of sinners, for peace between nations, for the sick and the dying, for the indifferent and the tempted, for the dead. I pray also for those who have asked me to pray for them at any time, and whose intentions I cannot now remember. Lord, take up before your throne the enormous list which comprises my prayer-obligation. In these terms I entrust my responsibility to you. I know that if I set myself to pray cause-by-cause and person-by-person, I shall end by presenting you with a catalogue instead of with a prayer. My aim is to worship you in spirit and in truth, and I know that nothing gets so effectively in the way of this as the effort to remember. Enough that the intellect has known what was proposed, and that the will has sanctioned the proposal; no need for the memory to strain itself or for the imagination to work up scenes and situations.

No need, either, for many words. So long as words flow easily, and so long as they genuinely express what is in my mind and heart, I shall feel no scruple in using them. But on the other hand, if I can unite myself to you in praise without them, I need feel no scruple in leaving words aside. Let me so yield myself to the grace of this sacrament that the prayer of love may be the main concern, and that the prayer-form may be secondary.

THE CHIEF OBSTACLE to the right reception of this
sacrament is not, as we are inclined to think it is,
routine. The chief obstacle

✠   CONFESSION   is want of trust. Without
much difficulty we can
turn the harmfulness of routine into the meritorious channel of good habit. But unless we have
trust we cannot come to a true state of contrition
or form a true purpose of amendment. Without
complete trust in God we shall find ourselves falling back upon some sort of trust in self, and when
we have discovered from experience how untrustworthy we are we shall be at a loss. Lord, let me
see that you are my whole strength, and let me
place my confidence in no other power but yours.

If I can come to see this sacrament more in
terms of God's mercy and less in terms of my emotional remorse, I shall be seeing it more from the
point of view of what he does than of what I do:
the important thing in all the sacraments is his
action rather than mine. Moreover I cannot count
upon my own emotional remorse, whereas I can
count upon his mercy. On one day I shall feel more
sorry than on another; about one sin I shall feel
more sorry than about another. But God's mercy
is *there*, the same on all days and extended to the
forgivenness of all sins: the one condition is repentance.

But how, if my feelings give no certain guide, do
I know that I have truly repented? I know this

when I can say that I have truly turned away from the sin in the will. I know this when I am prepared to avoid the occasions of committing the same sin in the future. I know this when I shrink from the idea of offending God's love, of contributing to the sufferings of Christ's passion, of being unfaithful to grace and ungrateful for countless pardons in the past. This is true repentance: the turning of the soul away from sin and towards the light of God's love. Every confession is a conversion. It is a revolution of the will. The desires come full cycle, back again to God where they belong. In this process of circulation, where the course of the mind is acting in harmony with the flow of grace, there may or may not be a scorching sense of shame and guilt. If there is, and it is certainly not an emotion to be belittled, it is to be submitted in all humility as a token of penitence.

If it is not my tears but Christ's wounds that bring me the pardon for my sins, neither is it my resolution but Christ's promise that gives me confidence as regards the future. Lord, you have pledged yourself to see me through the temptations which by myself I am too weak to overcome. I am so weak that there are some temptations which I do not seriously fight against, let alone succeed in overcoming, and it is against these that I particularly ask your help. I may know all about the distinction between necessary and unnecessary occasions of sin, between voluntary and involuntary acts, but

13

in the heat of temptation none of these divisions makes the smallest difference to the violence of my desire. It is then that I am weak all over, blind and stupid and selfish and ungrateful. It is then that I shall need the outpouring of your grace. This it is that I call for now in advance. I am sorry for my failures in the past because they have caused you pain; I will try to do better in the future because you want it so. I know no other formula for confession. Whatever is wanting, Lord, from your infinite merits please supply.

THOUGH BENEDICTION does not rank in excellence with the Mass, which is a sacrifice, nor yet again with the Holy Eucharist, ✝ BENEDICTION which is a sacrament, it enshrines elements of both and even the implications of both. Where the Mass is the act of Christ, a movement and a prayer, Benediction is rather a fact. Where the Holy Eucharist is Christ's bodily presence imparted, together with his soul and divinity, to the whole of man, Benediction is the same sacramental presence of Christ exposed to one of man's senses for his devotion and worship. Benediction is the ceremony which exhibits Christ before our eyes so that we may acknowledge his objective presence and pay homage in front of it. It is as though the elevation were taken from its liturgical and sacrificial setting in the Mass, and extended for a more prolonged adoration.

Lord, show me how to make the most of Benediction. Let it be both a continuation of my Mass-prayers and a renewal in spirit of my eucharistic unions. The grace which comes to me from the sacred Host in the monstrance is not the same as that which I receive when you come to me at the altar-rail but it is still a holy communion: my spiritual communions are not as sacramental and immediate as my actual communions, but at least they bring praise to your name and at the same time make me realize the closeness of your presence. In my acts of worship at Benediction I may not be able to receive you sacramentally but at least I can visit you in the Blessed Sacrament, and there unite myself with you. I may not be able to sacrifice with you as at Mass but at least I can offer myself to you as I do at Mass, and sing before you in union with the blessed who sing before you in heaven.

But there are other lessons to be learned from Benediction besides those that are strictly eucharistic and devotional. For example, I can remind myself that just as the body of Christ is exposed for veneration in the monstrance, so the spirit of Christ is enshrined for recognition and edification among the faithful—in me. There rests with me the alarming responsibility of showing to others the ideal and practice of Christ. My fellow Christians, and perhaps even those who are not Christians, should be able to see in the principles which

15

I hold, and in the conduct which verifies the sincerity of those principles, the authentic message of the Incarnation. I am not the word of the Gospel, but my life must proclaim the Gospel. As the sacred Host is held up by the priest as he blesses the congregation at Benediction, so Christ's example is upheld by me as I mingle every day with the congregation of men and women in the world. What if I fail to uphold that example? What if people see only me, and see nothing of him who is claimed by me to be my life and my inspiration? Benediction is not the monstrance.

Nor is Benediction the singing. Nor is it, if there is one, the sermon. Those who go to Benediction for any other thing than giving glory to God, and receiving from him the grace of increasing in his service, might just as well watch the ceremony on the screen. Lord, may you who are the way and the truth and the life so draw me to your presence at Benediction that love alone may be the attraction. Whatever other incentives there may be, it is on the motive of love that I want my Benedictions to be founded.

WHAT FOLLOWS IN THIS and in the ensuing section on the rosary will not be prayer-material so much as headings for suggested prayer-material. It is hoped that the soul, given the lead, will follow up with personal considerations and ejaculations.

✝ STATIONS OF THE CROSS

CONDEMNATION. Pilate had no clear knowledge of the issues at stake; I have. Pilate did not believe the warning signs; I do. Pilate could not draw upon the Scriptures, the Church, the sacraments for help; I can.

ACCEPTANCE. The cross was not forced upon Christ; he had offered himself for it and was waiting for it. The nearer I can get to this attitude of willing co-operation with the Father's will, the truer my likeness to Christ.

FIRST FALL. If Christ had had any strength left, he would not have fallen. This was no make-believe fall. He allowed his physical powers to fail him so as to be like me in all things, even in weakness.

MARY. If I want to know the place of suffering in the Father's scheme of human life, I can look at the souls to whom he sends it. The meeting between Christ and his mother is the saddest meeting in history.

SIMON. The idle spectator is made to be an active participant. Reluctance would have turned away the grace and spoiled the whole thing. But because there was willingness, a whole train of graces followed.

VERONICA. No idle watching here, but ardent compassion. The test of sympathy lies in the readiness to serve. Not only was Veronica's sympathy verified by her service, but her service was verified by its miraculous reward.

SECOND FALL. Christ fell twice so as to show us

that by repeated failure our perseverance is proved. After one fall we can persuade ourselves that it was an accident. After two we are inclined to lose confidence. Christ fell twice to *give* us confidence.

THE WOMEN. The teaching here is that of directed intention. Mourning must be supernaturalized. No sorrow, and least of all the sorrow that springs from charity, may be wasted. Tears of warm emotion can be turned to tears of true penitence.

THIRD FALL. Three times Christ exposed a physical inability to meet a demand. He allowed this limitation to be imposed upon his body so that we might contrast it with the unlimited reserves of his heart and will. It was only his sacred flesh that faltered; his love stood firm.

STRIPPING. Christ had a right to everything. He owns the world. Especially he had a right to dignity. He is himself perfect purity. But he was stripped of everything. He was left with nothing but shame.

NAILING. With him the nailing was inevitable only because he willed it so. With us it is circumstance that keeps us to our cross. But though we cannot escape it, we too can will it so. And herein lies our sanctity: with Christ we are nailed to the cross in obedience to the Father's will.

DEATH. The consummation of his life is seen in the consummation of his death. Here is perfect obedience, perfect love. The Word has said all.

Perfect soul leaves perfect body in a darkness which covers the whole earth, and in meekness and silence. It was the way in which he had come.

DEPOSITION. Mary's place in the nativity is reflected in the act of atonement. She has brought Christ into the world; she stands by while he takes his leave of it. If his own rejected him, they have still his own mother to plead on their behalf.

BURIAL. Instead of being the symbol of finality, the tomb is for us the emblem of hope: out of it rises our only hold upon eternal life. Christ's passion is our merit; his death and resurrection are our trust.

MARY, BEFORE I START upon the consideration of the mysteries of the rosary I ask you to help me

✠ THE ROSARY

in expanding and developing the ideas submitted below. Widen for me their application so that I may find myself praying for the whole world, and deepen for me their meaning so that my whole life may be lived at the level of their implication.

ANNUNCIATION. As Mary received her vocation without preconceived notions about what her vocation ought to be, so I must try to dispose myself for whatever work it is that God may want of me. In Mary's attitude I see at once the secret of holiness. *Ecce*—look—it is an open secret. If I can shape my life according to Mary's *Fiat mihi secun-*

19

dum verbum tuum I have found the answer to my soul's problem.

VISITATION. Sanctity is not sitting still and hugging the formula of sanctity. Mary's visit to Elizabeth before John's birth is the practical expression of an inward grace. Outward charity sets the seal to the movements of interior love. Elizabeth recognized this, and recognized too in the unborn Christ the principle of love itself.

NATIVITY. The Word was made flesh and came amongst us—in silence and while the night was in its course. In order to understand the Word I shall need to wait for it in silence, subduing the voice of the world which deafens. In order to see what the Incarnation means I shall need to look in faith, undismayed by the darkness of the world which hides it. Lord, you who are Word and Light, come to me across the waste land which separates my soul from your birth.

PRESENTATION. The mystery of oblation. With Anna, with Simeon, with Joseph and Mary, and finally with you, I offer myself to the Father. I renew the dedication of my baptism. I renew the offering which I make when I hear Mass. I renew my resolutions and offer again to you the intentions for which I have been asked to pray. Lord, take all.

FINDING. In Mary's anxiety at the loss there was no panic. There can be panic only where there is not perfect confidence in God. Lord, teach me to trust. I must know that whatever happens you are not lost to me, and that even your absences denote the Father's business.

AGONY. While the main work of reparation is being done for me, I am nevertheless called upon to make my contribution. I am asked to watch and pray while the agony is endured. Can I not watch even one hour with you, Lord? I pray that you may make me more alert.

SCOURGING. We each have our particular pillar to which we are tied. Most of us are lashed behind our backs by criticism. Lord, may your example reconcile me to being bound and torn to shreds.

CROWNING. The malice of ridicule is harder to bear than the malice of serious attack. Lord, from the mock homage that was paid to you let me learn to endure the pain of being made to look a fool.

CROSS-BEARING. In every hardship there are two elements: the physical and the mental. Let me learn from the hideous publicity of the way of the cross that humility is even more important than outward endurance.

CRUCIFIXION. Meekly bowing down his head, he gave up the ghost. All was consummated. Lord, not until the Father's will is fulfilled let me be allowed to give up. Then, in meekness, let me surrender to death.

RESURRECTION. The triumph over sin and death. The vindication of love. Hate and evil may compete but they cannot win. *Alleluia.*

ASCENSION. The crowning act which leads redeemed mankind before the Father's throne. Let me live in the knowledge of this, in the hope of this.

PENTECOST. At the nativity he came in the flesh, at this feast he comes in the spirit. The same love, the same wisdom, the same way and truth and life. Lord, let me receive you with the same worship.

ASSUMPTION. If it is one of the consequences of his sin that man should know decay, that his dead body should return to the dust from which it came, then Mary must escape the liability. The doctrine of the Assumption follows that of the Immaculate Conception.

CORONATION. Mary who in spirit shared with Christ the crowning with thorns shares now the crowning in heaven, and because the blessed enjoy her blessedness they enjoy also the same crowning of her merit.

JOINING WITH ALL THE FAITHFUL, and echoing the praise sent up in prayer since man first paid you homage, I submit to you my

✠ A LITANY litany and ask your blessing upon the intentions there expressed.

Holy Trinity one God—*We adore you.*

Father of mankind, Creator of the World—*Keep charge of us.*

Redeemer of the world, the Word and the Truth—*Keep charge of us.*

Spirit of wisdom and love, the Paraclete—*Keep charge of us.*

Mother of God—*Pray for us.*

St. Joseph—*Pray for us.*

The Twelve Apostles—*Pray for us.*

St. Mary Magdalen—*Pray for us.*

St. Augustine—*Pray for us.*

St. Gregory—*Pray for us.*

St. Bernard—*Pray for us.*

St. Bede—*Pray for us.*

St. Anselm—*Pray for us.*

St. Thomas of Canterbury—*Pray for us.*

St. Thomas More—*Pray for us.*

St. John Fisher—*Pray for us.*

The English Martyrs—*Pray for us.*

St. Benedict—*Pray for us.*

St. Francis—*Pray for us.*

St. Dominic—*Pray for us.*

St. Ignatius—*Pray for us.*

St. Teresa of Avila—*Pray for us.*

St. Teresa of Lisieux—*Pray for us.*

St. John Baptist Vianney—*Pray for us.*

St. John Bosco—*Pray for us.*

All saints in heaven—*Pray for us.*

All angels in heaven—*Pray for us.*

From the spirit of worldliness—*Lord, deliver us.*

From division and heresy—*Lord, deliver us.*

From the enemies of the Church—*Lord, deliver us.*

From persecution, famine, and war—*Lord, deliver us.*

From deceitful leaders—*Lord, deliver us.*
From temptation and despair—*Lord, deliver us.*
From pride and blindness—*Lord, deliver us.*
From all evil—*Lord, deliver us.*
For saintly bishops and priests—*Hear our prayer.*
For vocations—*Hear our prayer.*
For the welfare of the Pope—*Hear our prayer.*
For zeal among the faithful—*Hear our prayer.*
For the missions—*Hear our prayer.*
For a good Catholic press—*Hear our prayer.*
For all religious orders—*Hear our prayer.*
For sinners and tempted—*Hear our prayer.*
For the sick and dying—*Hear our prayer.*
For the poor and afflicted—*Hear our prayer.*
For the dead—*Hear our prayer.*
Lamb of God—*Have mercy on us.*
Sacred Heart—*Have mercy on us.*
Lord of understanding and love—*Have mercy on us.*

THROUGH THE THICKET of self-justification which I have allowed to grow up between myself and my

✠ **EXAMINATION OF CONSCIENCE**

guilt I must try to see the truth: I must face the evidence of my sins, must acknowledge the dangers to which my self-deception has made me liable, must humble myself before God and ask both for pardon and for help to be more honest with myself—as well as with him—in the future. Perhaps my evasions and excuses have offended

24

him more than my glaring failures. Open and admitted sin is bad enough, but worse is to call evil good and to pretend that bitter is really sweet. Leaving the question of the more obvious sins which appear on the surface of my conscience, I want now, by the light of a more penetrating grace, to examine the evils of my nature which tend either to escape the ordinary textbook classifications or else to disguise themselves as virtues.

Have I tried to convince myself that those qualities which I judge to be reprehensible in others are laudable when I see them in myself? Do I give myself the credit for being forthright and firm, for example, where others are harsh and pig-headed? Is my own meritorious flexibility (whereby I am "all things to all men" with St. Paul) any different from the double-faced behavior which I attribute to others? Am I the tactful and discerning lover of peace where others are hypocrites, moral cowards, men of compromise? Am I the long-suffering soul who is forever bearing the burdens of others in a spirit of charity, and is everyone else tainted with self-pity? Are my resentments due to my sense of justice while other people's resentments are due to their own native bitterness and selfishness?

On those occasions when I know I have failed do I acknowledge my guilt, or do I find reasons which explain the whole thing? For instance, do I put down the lapse to nerves, exhaustion, the effect of over-generosity in God's service? Am I hiding behind my practices of penance and prayer, imagining that they let me out of the practice of virtue?

Have I virtually rationalized sin, my own and even sin in general, looking upon it as inevitable? Have I come to tolerate sin in myself as being part of my physical and temperamental make-up? Have I come to accept it as admittedly a weakness but a weakness which cannot be very blameworthy because everyone else in the world seems also to suffer from it? Have I allowed the prevailing theories of non-Christian psychologists with regard to sin to carry weight with me? Have I come to look upon the duty of self-control as a frustration, and upon the warning of conscience as an inhibition?

Do I resent those impulses of grace which show me up for what I really am? Do I smother the voice of conscience with the voice of my lower self which argues that the line I am taking is not too unsatisfactory after all? "I may not be a saint, but I am not as bad as some; I am reasonably safe." Or this: "I have gone along like this for years, and have got no worse. Why should I make a change?" Or, and in some ways more dangerous because more defeatist, the attiude: "I doubt if I could make a change now anyway."

Lord, keep in me a lively sense of sin and a lively sense of grace. "The greatest sin of our generation," Pope Pius XII has said, "is that it has lost the sense of sin." Lord, that we may see.

RESOLUTIONS MAY NOT GUARANTEE results but it is hard to see how results can be obtained without resolutions. If I am to expect results from my resolutions, I must resolve according to grace and not according to caprice. Attaching to this matter of making resolutions there are two important conditions: the first is that I depend more upon God than upon my strength to carry them out, and the second is that I do not cramp myself with a multitude of resolutions which I shall not be able to keep. The value lies in the quality and not in the quantity. I may have any number of good desires, but I would be unwise to make resolutions about all of them. The fruitfulness of my desires depends more on a few effective resolutions than upon many ineffective ones. Better not to resolve at all than to resolve upon a course which stands little chance of being followed.

Lord, guide my spirit by the Spirit of Wisdom itself. So operate through my intelligence that I may decide upon the best practices to adopt. Show me the directions which need investigating, and dictate to me the terms which I am to impose upon myself. I want my will to be so informed by your will that my resolutions may be inspired by you, maintained by you, directed to the praise of your name and the good of my soul. Tell me exactly what steps to take so that my faults may be corrected and my spiritual life advanced. I promise to be obedient to whatever you demand of me and to accept all that you permit to happen to me. This indeed is my first and most comprehensive resolution: to be in every circumstance of my life submissive to your will. I mean to be ready not only to suffer your will but also to look for it. I pray to be shown what it is that you want me to do, and at the same time to be given the strength to carry it out.

Without burdening myself unduly, or tying myself up in knots, I can safely assume that grace is moving me to a more continuous prayer and a more extended charity. I do not lay myself open to scrupulosity if accordingly I resolve upon developing, with the help of grace, the habit of recollection. I will try to recall the presence of God during the day, knowing that this presence is all the time within me and all about me. At intervals in my work, in my recreation, and during those times when nothing particular is going on, I will try to turn my soul towards God in acts of worship. I am not here resolving to pray for long, because time may be against me, but I am resolving to pray more than I do at present.

In the same way, without fear of introspection, I can resolve to go further along the way of charity than the stage at which I now find myself. I know that this purpose has the help and blessing of Love itself. My resolution is accordingly to think more of the needs of others and to try to meet those needs

28

wherever I reasonably can. This means making allowances for people who think differently from myself, and trying to enter their minds so as to share their point of view. It means refusing to look for the flaws in others, and refusing to be put off by such flaws as may be evident. It means, whatever the disappointments suffered, believing in people; it means believing in every person. I resolve to do this. I have the grace to do it: it is God's will.

The resolution that has charity as both its impulse and its object can rely upon the force of charity to support its effort and crown its achievement.

IF I CAN COME increasingly to realize the apostle's doctrine *caritas Christi urget nos* I shall not only see my way to God but know

✠ CHARITY

that I am being propelled along it. On the other hand, if I do not allow charity to be my motive, I shall not only be in darkness but be left to myself to get out of it. My life without charity is nothing. God is charity, and to be without charity is to be without God. Charity is "the bond of perfection," is that which gives virtue to the virtues. And if it is Christ's charity which "urges us," it is Christ's perfection which perfects us. We have no charity of our own apart from Christ's; we have no perfection of our own apart from Christ's.

What in the practical field does this charity amount to—this charity of Christ's which must be mine as well? First it involves placing the Father's will before any other consideration whatever. This was in the mind of Christ, and this must be in my mind also. This is the first duty of Christian charity: to love God above all things. It means choosing the known will of God, whether signified through the commandments or through the Gospel or through the Church or through the light of conscience, in preference to every conflicting demand. The conflicting demand may be inside myself, coming in the form of personal inclination and natural passion, or it may come from outside in the shape of incitement to evil, pressure of circumstance, bad advice and worldly persuasion. God's voice alone commands my complete submission.

In human relationships the law of charity is often less clear but no less absolute. How can we pretend that we love God, is St. John's unanswerable argument, if we refuse love to God's representatives? If we claim to love the Father whom we do not see, we must verify our claim by showing love for his sons whom we do see.

And what, in practice, does this mean? It means forgiving those who have injured us. This, in the terms of the *Our Father,* is the condition of charity whether seen as worship or as Christian kindness. It means exercising compassion, consideration, trust. It means more than just being fair; it means being faithful. It goes beyond the legal requirement. On the negative side it means not finding fault, not yielding to suspicion and rash judgment, not stirring up animosities or dwelling upon imagined slights, not keeping up feuds and grudges, not allowing malicious gossip as an accepted social convention, not saying things that are calculated to hurt, not enlisting ridicule as a weapon, not parading a dislike, not condoning the uncharity of others. Snobbishness, bad temper, ill-natured criticism and nagging correction, neglect where charity is due, evasion of responsibility, assumption of superiority: all these and a hundred more are offenses against the love which we owe to one another and for which we are given the grace to exercise towards one another. Charity must be allowed to flow among the members of Christ's body; the circulation must never be allowed to slow down, still less to cease. Where there is unwillingness to exchange charity, the veins are virtually cut. Every cell in the body must be ready to meet every other cell in the name of the head of the body and in his terms.

All that is contained in this book of prayers, or indeed in any book of prayers, has no other aim but to further the life of charity. The soul who prays according to charity has found the way to God; the soul who lives with others according to charity has done the same.

JUST AS THERE is the true humility which reflects the humility of Christ, so there is a false humility which reflects the pride of the devil. There is the danger that if we go by the external signs alone in our assessment of humility we shall mistake the one for the other. The devil can pretend to the meekness of Christ. But he cannot pretend forever: false humility is disclosed on the touchstones of charity and obedience. "Learn of me for I am meek and humble of heart," says Christ, and if we put on the whole Christ—learning to love with his charity and to be obedient unto death with his obedience—we shall come to see the difference between the counterfeit and the true. "There is one that humbleth himself wickedly," says Ecclesiasticus, "and he is full of deceit." It is the proud man who wants to be thought humble; the humble man wants to be forgotten. It is easy enough for the proud man to speak softly and give the impression of great modesty and reserve. It is impossible for the proud man not to want to give an impression of some sort. The humble man wants to give no impression at all.

✠ HUMILITY

There is a school of thought which teaches that frequent exercise in humble works can beget humility of heart. A more sure approach would be to aim immediately at the humility of Christ in prayer. The exercise of humble works inevitably follows. To do the works without the purity of intention which is created by humility might be to strengthen the external to the neglect of the internal. To acknowledge complete dependence upon God, on the other hand, and to pray for the grace of humility without which every other virtue must be held suspect, is itself the disposition of humility. Humility, whether it is felt as a virtue or not (and indeed it is not likely to be felt), has then already begun.

Accordingly, Lord, I come direct to you as my model and my source of strength and light. I may learn something from rules of restrained behavior, from meditation-books which show me the folly of pride and the beauty of meekness, from reading about the humble practices of the saints; but I shall learn much more by laying my soul open to receive the communication of yourself. I do not ask to have the sense of humility, which may amount to no more than a sensation like any other, but rather to have the spirit of it. I know that it is not a virtue which will afford me much comfort, but I have not come to ask for comfort. It may even cause me much shame, and this is perhaps what my proud nature most needs. So long as what I see by the light of humility does not lead me to discouragement but rather to increased confidence in the power of grace, I shall know that I am not deceived by the false humility of the devil. Humility brings light, and I ask for light—however painful and humiliating. By the light of humility I can come to see truth. I may not come to see my humility at all, and it is far safer that I should not, but by its light I shall be able to find my way to other virtues, to other souls, to you. Without humility I shall never find my way anywhere.

However costly the process, let this education in humility be experimental and not academic merely. "Thy humiliation shall be in the midst of thee," says the prophet Michaeas. It is not put on like a cloak. It develops inside — in the measure that Christ's humility is allowed, together with his other virtues, to develop in the soul.

LIKE MEEKNESS, patience can be easily misunderstood. If the word "patience" has come down in the world, has come to signify a placid and perhaps spiritless calm, at least the virtue must not be devalued. Patience is something positive, is a strength. It may get its name from passive suffering, but it gets its power from active co-operation with the will of God. True Christian patience means active co-operation with the Passion of Christ.

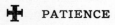 PATIENCE

Though natural temperament plays its part, patience is more than either inborn gentleness or studied composure. It is self-possession in the highest sense: "in patience you shall possess your souls." It not only has a supernatural object and value, but is absolutely necessary to the supernatural life of the soul. Without patience we cannot endure.

Without patience we cannot recognize the cross when we see it, much less carry it to the greater glory of God. But the cross is there in our lives and we must learn to see it as such. We must learn, through the virtue of patience, to bear it in union with Christ. Patience is not merely a virtue which serves very well for those who have an attraction for it, a virtue for some and not for others. If the Christ-life means anything to us at all it means that Christian patience is a necessity.

"My heart hath expected reproach" sings the psalmist. I await it as part of my God-given lot in life, as part of my inheritance. I rise to meet it, not in resentment but in patience. I go towards reproach and injury. Physically and emotionally I may shrink; in the will I accept. Patience is a matter of the will. There is nothing limp or supine about this virtue. It is as robust as fortitude of which it is a part.

Help me, Lord, to correct the obvious offenses against patience — irritability, fussiness, violence, anger, excitability—but more significantly let me have both the light and the strength to deal with the more subtle attacks upon this virtue. I must know that the truly patient man does not make excuses, does not try to escape, does not play the martyr, does not cry out against life or mumble about injustice. The patient man does not complain about being misunderstood, does not compare his trials with the apparently lighter trials of other people,

35

does not look back with useless longing to the happier days when his patience was not so severely tested. The patient man bears all things in unquestioning charity, endures all things with Christ. In fact, if he is perfectly patient he gives thanks for the opportunity which is given to him of proving the quality of his love.

How, without having to suffer affliction, can the soul ever come to a practical understanding of the Passion? It is only in patient acceptance that value and merit can be judged. Commenting on the verse in the Canticle which speaks of the soul as a "lily among thorns," St. Albert the Great says that "though it be pierced by thorns, the lily both retains its whiteness and sends forth a scent which is all the more pleasing for the piercing it has suffered." So the soul, crushed by adversity, sends out to God and to man the fragrance of patience under trial.

Lord, let me possess my soul in patience. Not in my patience, but in yours. Looking forward to eternal life, let me in the meantime endure with you my share in the sufferings of your sacred Passion.

IT MAY BE TAUTOLOGICAL to say that no virtue can survive where perseverance is wanting, but the thought is an alarming one nevertheless. Not even charity itself will secure eternal life to the soul if it is abandoned. Charity is the bond of perfection but the bond requires the final seal of perseverance or it ceases to

✝PERSEVERANCE

bind. However elaborate the plan for perfection, however painstaking the approach, however ruthless the renunciation of counter attractions, if the quality of perseverance is absent the whole thing must come to nothing. "Be thou faithful until death" we read in the Apocalypse, "and I will give thee the crown of life." This is our hope. But there is warning when the promise is read negatively, and the warning is as true as the promise. Without fidelity there can be no coronation.

The same note of warning is struck in a verse from the book of Proverbs where the wise man says that "there are ways which appear to men right, but whose end is in the depths of hell." The right way can be trodden but if it is trodden only for a time it might just as well not be the right way at all. Lucifer was in the right way but he did not persevere. Adam, you would have thought, was destined by the surest way to heaven. To Judas the vocation of apostleship was right enough, but he did not let it lead him all the way. Luther was a generous religious to begin with, but he tired of the obligations which he had undertaken. The way appears right when it is embarked upon, and indeed *is* right, but unless the man walking on it is faithful to its conditions until the end it leads him in the wrong direction.

Why is it that having successfully embarked upon a course which is clearly directly towards God, which has had God's blessing upon it, a soul can be so deceived as to turn away and give everything up? Is it always laziness or worldliness? Is it sudden collapse in the face of sudden overwhelming temptation? Certainly these things play a part in the soul's failure to persevere. Any one of them, or their combined influence, may constitute the immediate cause. But underlying all provocation to the abandonment of religion is lack of dependence upon God. The man who relies upon his own strength of character to carry him through to the end may well be left to his own strength of character, and this is not enough. We need grace to persevere. Final perseverance, so theologians tell us, is the gift of God. It is not something to which our strongmindedness entitles us.

Lord, I know that I can count upon your grace at every step of the way. I know that if I am faithful to this continued help I shall be granted the grace which marks the culmination. So far as I can I set my will to persevere, but at the same time I do not wholly trust my will. My trust is in you and not in myself. Experience has shown me, in my own case as in the case of others, that when men become too sure of themselves they neglect the supernatural. It is the supernatural and not the natural that will ensure my continued service to your name. Grant me, then, a lively sense both of the need to place my confidence in grace and of the threats to my perseverance which will accompany me right through life. I am safe only in so far as you keep me safe; I shall persevere only if you help me at every moment to persevere. I pray with confidence for the gift of final perseverance.

PERSEVERANCE IN THE SERVICE OF GOD is conditioned by the readiness to place oneself under the discipline of the will. My

✝ SELF-CONTROL constancy as a follower of Christ does not stand a chance so long as I allow myself to be at the mercy of conflicting desires as they follow one another in my heart. Relying always upon grace I must be able to say, with Job, that "I will not forsake my justification which I have begun to hold." My dependence upon grace assumes the willingness to accept discipline. The disposition for continued fidelity is found in the law of self-control.

In the ascending scale of self-control it is clear that the senses must be made subject to the spirit, and that the spirit must be made subject to grace. The body must be made to keep its place or it will prejudice the subjection of the spirit to grace. "We are debtors, not to the flesh to live according to the flesh," says St. Paul to the Romans, for "if you live according to the flesh you shall die." The body goes on making more and more demands, and if the will gives way there is an end to the life of grace. "Delicately treated flesh burns up and consumes the soul," says St. Augustine, "as fire burns up stubble." It is the life of the soul that is our main concern, and the sooner the body recognizes

39

this the better. If by the spirit we mortify the deeds of the flesh—this is St. Paul's and St. Augustine's doctrine—we shall live.

Lord, give me the strength to break those appetites, whether physical or emotional, which war against the all-important desire of my soul for you. Let me resist those pleasures which, by offering me the wrong sort of satisfactions of this world, have the effect of making me indifferent to the supreme satisfaction which is waiting for me in eternity. When you gave as the terms of discipleship that a man must "hate his own life also" if he is to come after you, you were telling me that to live in my redeemed nature with you involves the renunciation of my fallen nature as I might gratify it in the world. You were thinking not only of monks and nuns when you said that unless your disciple hate father and mother, and all human relationships, he cannot be your disciple. This vocation is extended to all Christians, and I may not evade its implications. How in this context am I to understand the word "hate"? What kind of service is expected of the "disciple"? Are all human relationships to be repudiated? Lord, give me light about these things, and in the meantime I can dwell upon St. Gregory's explanation of the passage where he says: "That which, by being spurned, is drawn on to something better, comes to be loved as it were through hatred."

If even good things are to be renounced in life,

then all the more strict must the soul be in the renunciation of the bad. The difficulty lies in the fact that the same radical renunciation cannot be applied all round. Show me, Lord, how in practice to exercise these renunciations and controls. Where the menace to my soul is an intrinsic evil, let me have the courage to cut it out and cast it from me. Where the evil is mixed with the good let me know how to destroy the one without spoiling the other. Lastly, since even good things can be enjoyed to excess or to the neglect of what is better, give me the wisdom to see all things in right proportion. Where grace is informing my essential self, the difficulty of self-control is solved. Control me, Lord, and I shall be self-controlled.

THOUGH THIS VIRTUE may not be numbered among the others as they appear in the lists, it nevertheless comprises  **SELFLESSNESS** quite a few virtues, and in any case is a quality to be prayed for. We know what we mean when we describe a person as being selfless, but it is difficult to find a definition which will cover the various aspects of the disposition which we have in mind. "There was a man in the land of Hus whose name was Job, and that man was simple and upright": perhaps this gets us as near to it as anything. The selfless man is uncomplicated and unreflective in his charity, and has no vanity to be fed by his acts of self-giving. The selfless man considers neither his own time, his own convenience, his own possessions or even his own reputation: his sole criterion is the love of God and the good of his neighbor.

In case this should suggest an attitude that is intemperate—a generosity so reckless as to have more of nature in it than of grace—we find a corrective in Christ's words to those whom he had summoned to an apostolate which was completely selfless. "Be ye therefore wise as serpents and simple as doves." Wisdom is here coupled with simplicity, suggesting that in the affairs of men wisdom without simplicity is cunning, while simplicity without wisdom is silliness. The selfless man is not the empty or shallow man; he is the man who is so filled with the spirit of Christ that there is no room for the spirit of self. When the object of a man's single-minded desire is Christ, the question of self-interest falls into the background. Self-esteem, vainglory, smugness, snobbishness—all this is forgotten. There is only one ambition, and this is to please God by furthering his interests in the world. There is only one fear, which is that God's interests may be badly served.

Lord, I pray that I may be given so great an attraction for this virtue that my native selfishness may find itself eclipsed. Show me from the example of your life on earth how to give myself unsparingly to the service both of the Father and of my fellow men. I know that if this change is to be effected in my character, I must develop a more earnest zeal for souls. Selflessness, as I see it in you and in those saints whose lives most closely resembled yours, must mean two things: first a great sympathy with the world, and second a great detachment from it. Grant me, Lord, a boundless confidence in human nature. Without inexhaustible funds of understanding and compassion I shall never come to the practice of selfless service to others. From the infinite store of your charity may I draw upon these virtues. But since sympathy without detachment might lead me into occasions of worldliness I pray also that I may be spared the lure of material things. It will not be easy to move among men and women of the world and still to keep only their best interests at heart. Nor will it be easy to render service to the world without thought of the rewards that my service may win. Just as my selflessness must be proof against the dangerous pleasures of the world and the compensations which the world offers, so I pray that it may be proof also against the zeal which looks for recognition and gratitude. Only when I can work for you alone, which will mean working in union with you and by the power which you alone can give, shall I be truly selfless in my work. In the place of my selfhood, Lord, give me yourself.

THE PERFECT EXAMPLE of confidence is to be found in Dismas, the good thief. Confidence is part faith and part hope, and it finds its impulse and end in charity. To know that the Lord has us in mind, and that in spite of our sins he will remember us in his kingdom, is to show confidence; to do so when the evidence of our senses tells us nothing of this, and when indeed the outward appearance would seem to point all the other way, is to reflect something of the confidence of the good thief.

✠ **TRUST**

Where lies our security? What are the grounds of our hope? Why do we bother to go on? When may we expect to see the results of our labor and waiting? Whom are we trying to please in all this? Confidence in the wisdom and providence of God, confidence in God's love, can meet these and their tributary questions. Confidence silences scruples, by-passes questioning and discussion, gathers strength and momentum as it turns one stumbling-block after another into a stepping-stone towards union with God. "They that hope in the Lord," says Isaias in his fortieth chapter, "shall renew their strength, shall take wings as eagles, shall run and not be weary, shall walk and not faint."

The Scriptures are ringing with acts of trust and with examples of trust vindicated. Noe, Abraham, Joseph, Josue, Daniel, Zorobabel, Judith and Job: all were souls of invincible trust in the ultimate realization of their hope. In the psalms the soul proclaims the trust which God in his turn guarantees: "I am with him in tribulation; I will deliver him and will glorify him." Even some who have been wanting in other virtues have been emphatic in their trust. "This everyone is sure of that worshippeth thee," says Sara the wife of Tobias to the Lord, "that his life if it be under trial shall be crowned; and if it be under tribulation, it shall be delivered; and if it be under correction, it shall be subject to thy mercy. For thou art not delighted in our being lost; and because after a storm thou makest a calm, thou pourest in joy after tears and weeping."

We have also the example of St. Joseph, who obeyed in perfect trust when he was told to take Jesus and Mary into Egypt. Commenting on this, St. John Chrysostom points out that St. Joseph might reasonably have argued thus: "You have said that he would save his people from their sins, and now he cannot even free himself from danger . . . that which has come to pass is in all points contrary to that which was promised." St. John Chrysostom reminds us that "nought whatever of this kind did Joseph urge, for he was a faithful man . . . he obeyed right willingly and believed, enduring with gladness every tribulation following."

Lord, let me take to heart the two last verses of the *Te Deum,* and mean in earnest what I am saying to you there: *Fiat misericordia tua, Domine, super nos; quemadmodum speravimus in te. In te,*

45

Domine, speravi; non confundar in aeternum. If I possessed the perfect trust which so often I proclaim, I would need to choose no new course of action, for you would do it for me. I would know that I could safely cast all care upon you, for you have care of me. I would be willing either to wait indefinitely or act at once, leaving it entirely to you to decide. I would know that you are more anxious than I am, Lord, to bring your work in my soul to perfection.

THE PRINCIPLES which we have been considering in relation to trust are never more necessary or effective than in occasions of

✝ SUFFERING

suffering. The sufferer will have to cling close to the beatitude, "Blessed are they that mourn for they shall be comforted," knowing that in human conditions true joy cannot be arrived at save through sorrow. "The Lord rules me and I shall want for nothing" is the psalmist's confident theme, "and if I should walk in the midst of death's shadow, I shall fear no evil." But to express this trust before the time comes is one thing, and it is quite another to show the same brave front when the suffering is actually present. The mark of true spirituality is gladness in suffering. This does not mean enjoyment of the cross, but gladness at being able to join with Christ in bearing the cross.

In this matter of suffering the difficulty for most of us is to avoid being sorry for ourselves when our sorrow might quite easily be raised above ourselves. Once united to the sorrows of Christ, our sorrows take on a new and supernatural meaning. The tragedy is not what we have to suffer but what we waste in suffering. We waste experience, we waste the chance of growing in compassion, we waste the best of all expressions of penance, but beyond even these opportunities thrown away we waste what is only waiting to be shared by the suffering Christ, by our Lady of Sorrows, by the suffering members of Christ's mystical body.

By hugging our grief to ourselves, letting it work inwards instead of outwards, we allow the grace of affliction to harm us where it is designed to help us. "A sorrowful spirit," we read in Proverbs, "drieth up the bones." By itself, without direction towards Christ and the sorrows of others, the spirit of sadness is a withering, shrivelling evil. Given its orientation in Christ, it is the most purifying and sanctifying factor in the soul's development. Religious men who are not Christians are sometimes more ready than we are to recognize the need and value of suffering. "Whenever heaven wants to confer a great work upon a man," wrote Mencius, an apostle of Confucianism, "it drenches his heart with bitterness, submits his nerves and bones to weariness, delivers his whole being to a great hunger, reduces him to extreme need, thwarts and upsets his enterprises. By this means it wakens in him good sentiments, fortifies his patience, and endows him with what has been lacking."

It is a curious fact that while we instinctively give more confidence to those who have suffered than to those who have not, we yet blind ourselves to the ennobling influence which suffering must have in our own case. Do we imagine that we can be ennobled, strengthened, purified without it? Suffering is the antiseptic or cauterization: without it we would go to pieces and rot.

Lord, I know that on this subject I can argue and advance illustrations till my brain no longer registers. The books are full of material proving the necessity and value of suffering. And the lives of the saints are full of examples. But the only book which I should need is the text of the Passion. Your own example should be enough for me. Teach me from the inspired words of the Gospel all that I must know about suffering. Give me from the cross the grace to put into practice what I learn. Let me live in spirit on Calvary, reproducing in my degree, the crucifixion which I see there. My experience of religion should teach me, and teach me experimentally, to "know Christ—and him crucified."

IT IS HARD TO DO WELL, Bishop Challoner observes, that which we can do but once. Certainly death is not something which we can practice beforehand. Yet in a sense we can go into training for it. We can condition ourselves to the idea, so that when the

✝ DEATH

time comes it will not shock us with the sense of horrible novelty. To the soul who has never given death a thought there must at the end be much to which he will have to adjust his mind. And in all probability his mind, at that hour, will be ill-equipped to adjust itself smoothly. In the nature of the case there are a thousand uncertainties about how we shall die, so as regards the surrounding circumstances there is nothing to be gained by the practice of forecasting possible alternatives. It is the two or three certainties, and not the many uncertainties, which should concern us during the years when there is no immediate threat of death.

The first and most obvious point is that the only reasonable security against a bad death is a good life. It would be presumption and not hope to assume that a sinful life stands as good a chance as a virtuous life when it comes to the grace of a holy death. If the love and mercy of God can be relied upon to operate outside their frame of reference as readily as they can be relied upon to operate inside it, why should he want us to keep out of sin at all? Why lay down the commandments if to break them has the same claim upon him as to keep them?

The second certainty is that we may not take risks on a margin of error: we must play for safety. Left to ourselves, always liable to lull remote and disagreeable realities to sleep, we shall gradually convince our minds that no danger exists and that a good intention must cover all. We can become vain in our imaginations, and our foolish hearts can become darkened, and our wisdom can be turned into deceit. Nor is it anything but folly and vanity to promise ourselves every sort of devout disposition at the hour of death when such dispositions are not attempted now while in health. Compunction, resignation, hope and love: these things cannot be switched on when the time comes without previous experience of their virtue. Right dispositions are graces from God, and to presume upon their possession on a given occasion while neglecting their possession in the normal run of life is to mock God who is the source of grace.

The third certainty is that we shall not be allowed to leave this life without some sort of struggle. Not many among the dead have spent their last days on earth in perfect peace of mind and body. If we have to fight while living, it is more than probable that we shall have to fight while dying. With these three considerations in mind I can now start praying about my death. Let my preparation for death, Lord, be the practical one of corresponding with your graces in the handling of my life. May I go to meet it open-eyed, not taking my chance on an easy pass but trusting in your grace to keep me well on the side of safety. And in whatever conflicts there may be at the end, I ask that you and your blessed mother and the saints may fight my cause and hold off from me the powers of evil.

I make mine the prayer of the martyr, St. Marinus, who prayed "See, O Lord, and help; give patience to me, that free from blame I may finish the race."

THE IMAGINATION is not more help to us in the matter of purgatory than in the matter of death.

✠ PURGATORY

Nor do the emotions bring anything to our consideration of purgatory—save perhaps a nervous dread. All we have to go upon are a few texts from Scripture, the doctrine and tradition of the Church, and the cold light of reason. But in fact this is more than enough. We can prepare for purgatory in the way that we prepare for death. In fact we can go further than in the case of death, because we can experience a foretaste of purgatory in a more real way than we can experience a foretaste of death. By ready suffering we can advance, so theologians tell us, the pains which are due for the purification of our souls. Since only the pure of heart may see God, there has to be a process of cleansing either here or hereafter. So why not, by willingly embracing the pains and sorrows of this life, begin the purgatorial process now?

Such was certainly the attitude of the saints during their time on earth. It was not because they thought to escape the more severe pains of purgatory that they chose the more immediate, and

51

softer, afflictions of the present. It was rather that their great longing to come to God, and to come to him without a stain on their souls, drove them to take the most direct course—which was through the trials of this life. In this spirit they were ready enough to take in their stride all the sufferings that came their way — or even sufferings that they could find. Seen thus, suffering to them was not an evil but a good, not a punishment but a privilege. And if there should be a purgatory still in store for them after their deaths—if after all there yet remained some punishment in store—why, that too would give them opportunity of further proving their love. "All that I suffer is nothing," protests St. John Chrysostom. "Oh, if you knew how God strengthens me. It is my delight to suffer for him whose love cannot grow cold. Soon I shall be with him forever."

We do not need to draw upon either the visual imagination or the emotion of fear to form a concept of the soul's state when faced, at the particular judgment, with the prospect of purgatory. Surely the knowledge that union with God is now assured will compensate for the temporal punishment and the delay. If even in this life the assurance which we sometimes experience that we love God and are loved by him can have the effect of blotting out all suffering, the same assurance confirmed and appreciated to an extent unattainable on earth must have the effect of making the fires of purgatory seem infinitely worth while. We are perhaps inclined to forget that the holy souls have had their glimpse of God, and the purpose of purgatory is not to make them forget this vision but rather to make them remember it so vividly as to suffer the pain of longing. The separation is not the agonizing separation of estrangement but the homesick separation demanded in the terms of love.

I shrink from pain, Lord, whether in this life or the next. Especially do I shrink from the pains which I do not know and cannot imagine. But in the uncharted land of purgatory I shall have the light of your face to guide me, and I place my trust in this. Give me the courage to start my purgatory here on earth, and grant me the grace of making the most of my opportunities. I pray also for all those souls now in purgatory, and for those who will be my companions when, as I hope, I shall eventually get there.

IF HEAVEN IS LOVE, hell is hate. Just as love in heaven is without the anxiety which we feel here on earth when we love—namely the

✠ HELL anxiety about not being able to prolong the love, about the lurking selfishness in its expression, about conflicting loves—so hate in hell is equally unrelieved. In this life when a man hates he gets a certain satisfaction from his hate. It may be a bitter and inverted satisfaction, but at least it releases a tension. In hell when a soul hates, and there is nothing else for a

53

soul to do but hate for all eternity, there is infinite bitterness but no satisfaction. When we think of hate we probably think of anger as either giving rise to hate or providing the appropriate medium of hate. But in hell there is nothing even as healthy as anger. Anger would be a diversion in hell, a distraction. In hell there can be nothing but slow, smouldering, hopeless, wasted remorse: despair, regret, and bitter loathing.

The first object of the damned soul's hatred is, of course, God. Knowing now without any shadow of the doubt which was experienced on earth that God is infinitely lovable, is love itself, the soul is possessed of a power which turns love inside out. The soul knows about infinite love but is shut off from infinite love. Is not only debarred from rendering any love at all but is compelled to render love's opposite. Unable to love back, unable to love anything or anyone else, unable to suppress desire and so remain neutral and suspended, the soul in hell can do nothing else but hate what is known to be the completely satisfying object of love. As the object of hate, God is not satisfying at all. The damned soul wishes that God could satisfy hatred, but is miserably aware that the longing for satisfaction, whether in love or in hatred, will go on forever.

But it is not only God that the soul hates. In hell every soul hates every other soul. Nor can there be the least comfort in the thought that evil is shared, that others have damned their souls too, that one is not alone in having chosen wrong instead of right. There can be no sense of fellowship in hell. Since souls were created to reflect God's image, every other damned soul is a standing witness to the malice which can turn what is lovable into that which is hated. If one soul in hell possessed some quality which could still be loved, there would yet be a chance: the others would turn to that soul in love and the soul would respond. But in hell there is no room for this. Charity has been put in reverse, and all are wholly hating and hateful. Malice reigns. If a single condemned soul could rid hell of the others and be alone in its hatred it would do so; having others there as hateful as itself makes it worse.

Finally the soul is filled with self-hatred as well as hatred for God and for others. Not with self-pity, which is a ministering sort of evil, but with self-hatred. Just as a man will hate himself on earth for wrecking his chances, so in hell a soul will see how culpably the grace of eternal life has been thrown away and will turn against self in reproach.

Lord, save me from going to hell. Give me such grace that I may steer my course wide of the way that leads to it. Remind me of the danger, and show me where my whole and only security lies. Let me not be like the foolish bridesmaids who ended up hating the bridegroom, their fellow guests and fellow bridesmaids, and finally themselves. It was not the bridegroom's fault that they were shut out; it was their own. Lord, show me from this parable that I cannot afford to take risks.

HAPPILY THERE IS NOT the same mystery about heaven as there is about hell. The Scriptures tell us more about it, theology tells us more about it, and we have the Church's authority for knowing that certain souls whose lives on earth we have been able to follow are actually there. Our own instinct, moreover, shows us that we are made for a love which cannot be fully met in this life and which only an infinite object can satisfy. Happiness in God is more real to us, and as an idea more native to us, than unhappiness in hell. The longing for eternal peace in Christ is, for the normal Christian, more constant than the dread of eternal torment in hell. Nevertheless it is for the normal Christian, as it is also for the Christian who makes high perfection his aim, to develop this longing. Keeping the eyes of his soul firmly on the goal of eternal life in heaven, the Christian will be able to walk among the things of this world without attaching himself too greedily to any of them. "Build not your house upon the bridge," says a Chinese proverb. We have a dwelling not made with hands which is in heaven, and until we enter upon our inheritance we are pilgrims and strangers in the land.

It is only by a right understanding of what is

promised that we can come to a right understanding of what is held. It is because we do not look enough at heaven that we flounder about here on earth. We hold material things too tightly; we are afraid to let them go. Seeing things in terms of years instead of in terms of eternity, we make for the quick return, the immediate pleasure, the expedient of the moment. Of course the thought of death is alarming to the man who thinks of it simply as a curtain coming down upon the stage. To the man who lives more or less habitually with the thought of heaven there is nothing disagreeable in the thought of death. He looks forward to it as the means to fuller life. "As to exile, the earth is the Lord's," sighs St. Basil, "while as to death, it will admit me into life." The same saint expresses the same idea in another place: "O Lord, thou hast taken away from us the fear of death; thou hast made the close of life the opening of a new and truer life."

Grant me, Lord, the focus of vision which you grant to saints. Let me look in faith and hope to what you are holding ready for me in heaven. Faith and hope, not imagination and feeling. "Eye hath not seen nor ear heard, neither hath it entered into the heart of man," says St. Paul to the Corinthians, "what things God hath prepared for them that love him." My whole business is to love you, Lord. Grant that I may so love you here on earth that the thought of loving you eternally in heaven will give the impulse to every work of mine, every human relationship, every ambition. And in every disappointment, trial, or sorrow, let the hope of heaven keep me from yielding to despair. In my heart I know that St. Paul's assurance to the Romans is true, that "the sufferings of this present time are not worthy to be compared with the glory to come that shall be revealed in us," but in my outward life, with its difficulties and sometimes heart-breaking upsets, I find the doctrine hard to remember and apply.

As a basis for my prayers on the subject of heaven I take two verses from the final chapter of the Apocalypse: "The Spirit and the bride say: Come. And he that heareth, let him say: Come. And he that thirsteth, let him come . . . let him take the water of life freely . . . Surely I come quickly. Amen. Come, Lord Jesus."

IT WOULD BE A MISTAKE for Catholics to judge that they had satisfied their obligation towards the Papacy when they had prayed for the Holy Father's intentions while gaining an indulgence. Nor does a coin in the box marked "Peter's pence" relieve the debt. If the Pope is the visible head of the Church on earth there should be a closer relationship between head and members than that which would exist in a social, political, or economic body. The Pope is a father and a shepherd as well as a pontiff; our attitude should be filial and depend-

✠ THE POPE

ent, therefore, as well as reverent. It would be unfilial on the part of a son to take no interest in his father, to avoid learning his father's views on current subjects, to listen without protest to criticism of his father's decisions, words, and private life. It would show an independent attitude on the part of the flock if shepherds of other flocks were sought out and listened to, if the sheep had their own ideas as to where to graze and what to feed upon. If we want to be fully functioning members of the Church as Christ left it in St. Peter's hands we shall need to give more than our formal obedience to St. Peter's successor. Whatever the claim of strict legal justice in the matter, Christ's Vicar is entitled in the name of ordinary piety and fittingness to the loyalty and devotion of the faithful.

If in our submission to the Holy Father we lived up to the belief which we profess—that all authority comes from God and that this particular authority is invested with special sanctity and special prerogative—we would never dream of denying the respect which is due. Our failure is not so much a failure of obedience as a failure of faith. It should be part of our virtue of religion as much as part of our duty as subjects to see in the reigning Pope the person and authority of Christ. While it is true that we must reverence the office even when the man who holds the office may be unworthy of reverence, it is also true that we must look for qualities in the man that are worthy of

59

reverence and not presume to pass judgment on those that seem not to be worthy.

Lord, I pray to be guarded against indifference towards this key position in your Church. I know how easy it can be for me to adopt an attitude of gentle mockery, of not-quite-sinful cynicism, of worldly superiority. This is sheer pride and a virtual negation of the supernatural. If among my fellow Catholics I want to appear well-informed and disillusioned about Vatican affairs, if among non-Catholics I like to be thought broad-minded and an independent thinker, I am treading on very thin ice. Grant me the humility to be not only obedient but delicately perceptive of the issue at stake. In bowing without reservations of any sort before you and your law, I bow also before your representative and your Church.

I pray, moreover, for the present Pope. May he receive your inspirations and graces with generosity; may he look to your wisdom for his direction more than he looks to the wisdom of men or to the signs of the times. Without your wisdom to guide him he will be unable to discern between one wise counsel and another, and he will misread the signs of the times. I pray then for the Pope's enlightenment, and I pray also for his health and spiritual good. May he find sanctity in your service, and be rewarded with a high place among the blessed.

To some it may come easier to give respectful obedience to the Pope than to the Church. The idea of the Church has an

 **THE CHURCH** impersonal, institutional, universal connotation. In being cynical about the Church a man may feel that he is doing nobody any harm; it is not like saying something behind a churchman's back. Yet the Church is the bride of Christ. Nothing could be more personal than that.

There are Catholics who imagine that the Church exists for the purpose of making rules and seeing that they are kept. But the Church is more than a legal and administrative body; it is the mystical body of Christ. It is more than a theological system and a moral arbiter; it is the mind of God expressing itself in human terms. If we want to know the truth about religious things, about what to believe and how to behave, we look to the Church to tell us. If we want to know what God thinks, we ask the Church and we get our answer.

There are Catholics again who would willingly obey the commandments of God, given to Moses on Mount Sinai, but who are less willing to show the same obedience to the commandments of the Church. The authority is the same, the voice which speaks through the Old Law is that which speaks through the New. The Word is the same, whether it comes by revelation, incarnation, or official interpretation. God is one; God is in the Church and

61

the Church is in God. In making divisions and reservations we offend against the unity of God and weaken the integrity of our response.

In our prayers we cry "Lord, that I may see," and when he shows us through his Church we do not look. If we expect a revelation we shall, of course, be disappointed with an order. We say "Lord, teach me how to pray," and when he gives us a new formula in the Church's liturgy we pick holes in it. Of course, if we have expected an inner light to instruct us in the secrets of devotion we shall receive without excitement the printed supplements which have to be stuck in at the back of our missal.

Lord, show me that there is no true obedience, either to the Church or to any lesser authority, where the subject dictates the terms of the precept. Show me that supernatural obedience to the Church and to superiors is founded on the desire to know your will and do it. Faith and humility are essential to obedience. Not my will, Lord, but yours be done. "He is thy best servant, O Lord," St. Augustine affirms, "who does not desire to hear from thee what he wishes, but rather wishes that which he hears from thee."

Teach me also, Lord, the essential relation between obedience and charity. Charity is what my soul craves for above all, while the attraction to obedience is not so keenly felt. I need to know, and to know experimentally, the truth to which St.

John bears witness when he says that "this indeed is charity, or the love of God, that we keep his commandments, and that his commandments are not heavy." Nothing can give me the happiness which I look for in you and in your charity but the faithful observance of your law as represented and expounded by your Church. This is true peace and true liberty, to be a loyal member of your Church.

I pray accordingly for the spread of the Church and for all its works. I pray for those of its members who are being persecuted, tempted, or exposed in any other way to suffering. May all in authority in the Church receive your light and blessing.

✠ THE WORLD   THE PRINCIPLE GOVERNING this subject is laid down by our Lord where he says in the Gospel of St. Matthew that "no man can serve two masters." Wherever the world comes in competition with the spirit it must be ruthlessly put back in its place or the dominion of the soul will yield to sense. The two demands cannot be balanced; one or other claim must go. The effort to square the conflicting desires—the one wanting to serve God, the other wanting to find happiness in material things—can result only in a tension which is almost as harmful to the soul as the surrender itself. Almost as harmful, because even if it does not yield outright to the world, it yields to the occasions of its sins; and it is certainly more hypocritical, since it keeps up the appearance of being faithful to

God. "Their heart is divided," testifies the prophet Osee to Israel's infidelity, "and now they shall perish." (And in the event, of course, this particular generation of Israel perished miserably.)

The theory is clear enough. It is stated by St. John in his gospel and his epistles: "Love not the world, nor the things that are in the world . . . if the world hate you, you may know that it hath hated me before it hated you." St. James says the same thing: "Know you not that the friendship of this world is the enemy of God? Whosoever therefore will be a friend of this world becometh an enemy of God." But how is this theory to be put into practice by people living in the world, by souls who do not happen to have the grace of a religious vocation which would keep them away from the world? The answer to this is to be found in looking at the above texts and noting the words "love," "hate," "friend," "enemy." In other words, for the man whose work lies in the world, and whose vocation calls him to family life, the question is not how much he is in the world but how much the world is in him. If, living in the world or in the cloister, a man *loves* the world and is its *friend*—if he accepts the world on its own terms and adapts himself to its standards—he is unworthy of his status as a Christian. The world has infiltrated; it has got inside him. But if, while still immersed in material concerns, he keeps his soul for Christ and abhors the spirit of the world, he will not be blamed at the judgment-seat of God for being worldly. In the Office which the Church gives to the feasts of virgins, the saints are described as "contemning the kingdom of this world and all its glory for the love of our Lord Jesus Christ."

Teach me, Lord, how to distinguish between the true and the false in all this, and how to avoid hypocrisy and special pleading. I know that the works of God's hands are good, that sinners must be loved, and that the Father "so loved the world as to send his only begotten Son into the world" to redeem it. But I know too that a misunderstanding of these truths can pave the way first to compromise, then to fraternization, then to complete identity with the world. Grant that without smugness I may be able to stand back from the scene and judge according to your light and not according to the ways of those who have made their concessions to worldliness and who want me to join them. Show me that as I must hate the sin and love the sinner so I must also hate the world and love the worldling. Show me, in short, how I may reproduce in my soul the attitude which was yours while living in this world.

SINCE NO MAN in his senses would choose to serve Satan rather than serve God, we must try to find out where the attraction lies ✚ THE DEVIL —so that when the occasion presents itself we may avoid it. If there were no attraction we would not be warned against it. If there were not such a being as Satan we would be warned only about the tendencies of our lower nature. Satan is not an evil myth, the personification of what draws man away from his true purpose. Satan has not been invented to frighten us off sin. Satan is a person, but always a person disguised. He possesses intelligence, but not a supernatural intelligence. He commands a greater knowledge than that enjoyed by human beings, but the knowledge is not infinite. And that is about all we need know of Satan.

The attraction to Satan is not to the being as he is in himself but to the false presentation of good which we see in him. We yield to his persuasion only because he persuades us to see something likeable in what he wants us to do. To those who are striving to walk in God's light, the devil appears as an angel of light. No saint would feel tempted by the devil unless the devil took care to disguise himself as a fellow saint. Himself a fallen angel, Satan appeals to the fallen angel in each of us. There is something about our nature since Adam's sin which has an affinity to something in the nature of Lucifer, the sinning archangel. In order to attract the worldling, Satan does not have to rise so high in his disguise as to wear the livery of angels. It would in any case be thrown away on the worldling. Instead he adapts himself and his technique to the medium which is likely to interest the man of the world. Where the sensualist, the gross sinner, is the object of Satan's enticements the response is elicited at the lowest level. But even here, where the bond between the devil and the sinner is frankly sin, it is always under some aspect of good that the temptation is presented. If there was nothing of good to be got out of the evil proposed, the tempted man would see nothing in it to desire. The main work of the devil, then, is to make the kind of offers to the kind of people who are most likely to accept them. Having gained their consent, and having consequently proved himself right in suspecting where their weakness lay, he comes back again and again to the same weak spot. That is why our sins tend to conform to a pattern. It means that the devil, his superior intelligence confirmed in our regard, is not wasting his effort over those defences of ours which are strong but instead is having it his own way where we have shown to him that we are ready to yield.

Lord, the power of grace is greater than the power of temptation. Whatever Satan's abilities, his scope and influence are limited by conditions imposed by you. Lord, I pray that when you see me weakening under his insidious attack — that subtle attack which is not open warfare but an invitation to a peace which is false—you may give me light to see the situation's deceit. Satan is a liar and the father of lies. You are Truth itself and the Father of souls who would be true. Support me in truth, surround me with truth, let truth be my shield of defence and my spear of attack. If I trust in you and not in my own wisdom, strength, experience, argument — indeed in any human force at all—I know that the powers of evil will not be strong enough to win me. *In te, Domine, speravi; non confundar in aeternum.*

SINCE NONE OF US is without pride and concupiscence, it is upon these two flaws in our nature that **✝ THE FLESH** the devil's interest is chiefly brought to bear. Whatever the discipline which we impose upon ourselves we still crave for independence and the satisfaction of our sensual appetites: the pride of the flesh has to be subdued by humility and obedience; the lust of the flesh by Christian chastity. In each case it is the positive cultivation of the virtue as exhibited to us by Christ that is the effective answer to our weakness. To stop short at correcting the vice is not only to limit the supernatural opportunity of the work but to leave room for introspection, scruple, and possibly also discouragement, reaction, and failure.

That the more sure way of subduing our lower nature is the indirect way of shaping our minds according to Christ can be verified in the experience of the saints. "Spiritual delights being once tasted," says St. Bernard, "all carnal delights are found to be insipid." St. Gregory teaches the same doctrine: "The soul can never be without delight. It is delighted either with the lowest things or with the highest; and with how much greater industry it aspires to the highest, with so much greater despising it turns away from the lowest. And with how much heat it is inflamed towards the lowest, with so much more tepidity it grows cold towards the highest. For both of them cannot equally be loved together."

"Blessed are the clean of heart," runs the sixth beatitude, "for they shall see God." In the process of keeping the heart clean there is a negative and a positive activity. The negative lies in the deliberate separation from all that may occasion sin; the positive in the directing of the heart's desire towards God. God is not mocked, and to hope for the fulfilment of the beatitude while remaining within easy reach of unnecessary provocation is an insult to divine love. If Jacob's daughter, Dina, had not allowed her curiosity to lead her into the occasion of sin she might have been numbered among the holy women of the Old Testament. To Noe and Lot were granted great graces, but these graces were not followed up because the pleasures of sense were not guarded against and controlled. Josue and David, on the other hand, though guilty of serious self-indulgence, were men who fought their weaknesses, did penance, and lived on in holiness.

Lord, I understand that if I am to overcome the flesh and inherit the promise of the beatitude I shall need to possess the single eye which you speak about in the Gospel. My outlook must be sincerely directed towards you; I must seek you "in simplicity of heart" as we read in the book of Wisdom. Give me grace to restrain the pride of life and the lust of the flesh. I know that the devil will make it his business to stir my mind to rebellion and my body to restlessness and wrongful desires. But I cry out to you, knowing that you can say the word and restore order in my soul. Be with me especially when power is put into my hands and when my affections are roused. Reveal to my soul more of your own dispositions than I understand or can appreciate at present: let your humility be my strength when the pride of corrupt flesh tries to assert itself, and may your purity be the ideal for me to follow when my natural appetites try to sweep away my principles.

SELF-DECEPTION IS SUCH that little by little we can so excuse our moral failures as virtually to explain away sin altogether. From giving ourselves the benefit of the doubt, we go on — supposedly in common charity — to give everyone else the benefit of the doubt. How can I blame others (we say with a fine show of broadmindedness and the laudable desire to avoid hypocrisy) when I do not blame myself? I have really come to doubt (we conclude) whether anyone is strictly guilty. We advance the effect of heredity, of certain glands, of environment, of education, of background, of health, of sheer inward

✠ SIN

compulsion. We decide that there must be enough in all this to let almost anybody out. It is not that we do not see sin; we do—but we give it another name.

There is a disease of the brain called *agnosia,* which renders the patient incapable of recognizing familiar objects. The sufferer from this complaint sees a piano or a bicycle, but cannot remember what the thing is for. He knows he has come across, and perhaps even used, what he is looking at. But it means nothing to him; its function has to be explained. The disease is, in its medical and psychological form, rare. But a sort of spiritual *agnosia* must be very common. We can see sin, whether in ourselves or in other people, and not recognize it. Its appearance is not strictly new to us—in fact, the trouble may lie in its very familiarity—but its essential meaning has been forgotten. Even when we have had it explained to us, we can again forget; we can go on not recognizing it for what it is.

Now sin is an offense against God. It is an insult to his love. It is the negation of our purpose. It is the misuse of our God-given faculties. It is the means of our destruction. It is that which merits for us the loss of God, of eternal life, of the satisfaction of every craving. Happiness and sin can never come to terms. Where there is sin there is no true peace, no true liberty, no true joy.

How, Lord, does my *agnosia* stand up to that? Do those statements still command my assent? Or do they pass before my eyes like the lighted signs of an advertisement and quite fail to carry conviction? I pray, Lord, that your grace may stir in me a belated sense of guilt, a sense of danger, a sense of sin's reality. Let me not give a mere notional assent to the Church's doctrine about sin, but let me conceive such a fear of it that when tempted to commit it I may back away in disgust. But let the fear be filial and not simply servile: let me dread to offend you even more than I dread being punished for yielding.

This tendency to become case-hardened, over-familiar with a familiar thing, can extend to many aspects of my religious obligation. As a spiritual agnosiac I can fail to recognize the significance of the Sermon on the Mount, of the miraculous element in the Church, of the liturgy, of the Passion and the Crucifixion. Lord, I can even fail to recognize you. I can look into the perfect law of liberty and then turn away and not remember what I saw. "If a man be a hearer of the word and not a doer," says St. James, "he shall be like a man beholding his countenance in a glass; he beheld himself and went his way and presently forgot what manner of man he was." His indifference bred forgetfulness. An extreme case. We must see ourselves as we are—guilty and all too liable to sin again—and not allow ourselves to forget what we have seen.

IF WE EXAMINE the devotional literature of almost any generation earlier than our own we shall find only passing references to self-pity.

✚ SELF-PITY

It does not seem to be treated as a vice of any standing, and we would have to go a long way to find a prayer directed against it. Perhaps in the older view there was little need to ask God to rid us of something which we could quite well get rid of by ourselves. But it would seem that in our own time the need does exist for prayers and meditations upon this subject: we need to enlist all the support we can in attacking an evil which can prove fatal to our spiritual response. Self-pity may not be able to destroy our faith or undermine our morals, but if it can take the heart out of our service it can do a good deal of harm. It may or may not be a specifically twentieth-century failing — though to judge from contemporary drama, fiction, autobiography, published letters and diaries, medical and psychiatric reports, it would certainly seem to be—but if it is one from which we happen to suffer it deserves attention here. We need to see it as material which must rouse the devil's liveliest interest, as material for what may easily grow to be despair. We must see it not merely as an unfortunate turn taken by suffering, but as an evil, a vice, a guilty thing and matter for confession. We must see it as something to be fought with every means at our disposal, as something to be feared and prayed against. We must ask God to deliver us from this danger which is all the more danger-ous because when we are deepest in its danger we are often least aware of it. Self-pity is a mood with a difference. Where the mood of exaltation or anger or laziness or homesickness can be recognized as a mood, the mood of self-pity can so far escape recognition as to become a settled habit. Few would be so misguided as to bear a grudge forever, as to indulge the vice of idleness forever, as to maintain an attitude of sullen inaccessibility forever, but there are many who can find a never-ending pre-occupation with their misery.

Lord, spare me from this ill-conceived melan-choly. Trials and sorrows are graces which call for co-operation and not for self-commiseration. Grant that I may not waste the chances of going out from myself to you. By self-pity I only burrow deeper into myself and away from you. Let me be always on the alert to detect this secret tendency —which is secret only to myself for it shows itself quite clearly to those who have to listen to my story. I pray that the disguises under which it op-erates may be whipped away, and that in your light I may see the subterfuges to which I have resorted. Show me that often when I talk about injustice I should be talking about my guilty resentment against what is just. Show me that when I adopt a martyred air and say with a brave, sad smile, "But then it is only what I deserve after all," what

I really mean is "Why should this happen to me of all people?" Show me how easy it is for self-pity to spread to persecution-mania, to disobedience, to pride, uncharity, sins against the state of life ordained by God, and ultimately even to the abandonment of the life of grace. I can reach the stage of culpable loneliness and despair when no other consideration will weigh with me but that of escape. Lord, I do not believe that self-pity is proper to my generation, but I do believe that now more than ever before we need to be guarded against it. I pray for the victims of it. I pray for myself—that it may never carry me to its possible consequences but that your grace may enlighten me in time.

WE NEED, if it is not to be a drag upon the spiritual life instead of a means towards rapid spiritual advance, to come to a decision  LONELINESS about solitude. To drift into it when the occasion comes our way, and then to drift out of it again with no clear idea of its possibility and purpose would be not only to miss an opportunity but also to provide occasion for discouragement. Most people, whatever their place in life, are faced at one time or another with periods of solitude, and if the dangers of loneliness are to be avoided a principle has to be established and a practical approach has to be evolved. Solitude and loneliness are not the same thing, but the way to the right handling of loneli-

75

ness is almost always through the right handling of solitude.

In the first place, solitude must be seen as a good and not as either an inescapable bore or a downright evil. A man must come to terms with solitude or the loneliness of it will crush him. He goes out to meet it, knowing that when he is alone he is more likely to learn the truth than when he is hearing about it from people. He will learn truth about God, about himself, and about creation. Nothing so clears the mind of unnecessary accumulation as loneliness lived in simplicity and faith. Material interests drop away and the world is seen for what it is. "Enter thou into the rock and hide thyself," urges the prophet Isaias, who knows that to be alone with God is the highest experience granted to man.

If solitude is thought of as physical isolation, and if loneliness is thought of as the hollow ache which longs for companionship, then certainly there is little encouragement in the prospect. With nothing to replace what is absent, the soul may well suffer uselessly when having to endure being cut off. Such a soul falls easily into listlessness, preoccupation with self, the habit of helplessness and even of hopelessness. But with prayer and the Christ-life to draw upon, why should the soul ever endure the sense of being cut off? To those who make the presence of God the supreme reality, solitude robs loneliness of its sting. If we looked at solitude for its opportunity instead of for its menace we would see what strengths it offers to the soul. Just as by voluntary poverty a man is made independent of luxury, and by voluntary chastity made independent of reciprocated affection, so by voluntary solitude a man can come to rise above half the adjuncts of life—adjuncts which seem so necessary but which are not. Few factors will teach a man so surely and so swiftly as solitude the vital lesson of detachment.

Lord, let me cease to think of loneliness as a sadness unshared and longing. Let me think of it rather as the disposition for closer union with you. If I shrink from being alone, Lord, it is a natural shrinking merely. Help me to get my emotions, my superficial reactions, under better control. And if in my actual experience of solitude I still feel miserable, let me try to direct my loneliness in the direction of your Passion. Remind me of that deep inner loneliness which was yours — a loneliness which had nothing to do with the solitude to which your sacred heart was drawn—when your love for man was rejected, when there was none except your own mother who understood, when you heard the cry go up from those whom you had come to save, "Not this man but Barabbas."

ONE MAN SEES RELIGION as a necessary burden, another sees it as a consolation. One man sees it as a collection of doctrines and laws, another as a relationship.

✠ THE AFFECTIONS

We see things largely through the lens of our individual natures. If we could manage to see religion more as Christ sees it, and less as it is framed by our own natural conceptions, we would not only fulfil its obligations with less fuss but also find peace in our surrender to its essential demand. The service of God might be described as the amplification of love: charity carried into all human experience, and all human experience deriving its character from charity. Our affections are accordingly to be viewed in the light of charity and not in the shadow of self.

Precisely because God is love does the devil make love the chief object of attack. Affections which have their place in the scheme of divine charity are drawn out from their proper context by the powers of evil and given a false impulse and direction. If the human heart were a neutral organ, of no great spiritual significance either way, then this question of controlling the affections would be as straightforward as that of controlling one's extravagance or one's reading. But the heart is by no means neutral: it is made for God and made for man, and must express itself according to God and according to the best, not according to the worst, of man's nature.

Lord, show me your ideal in my relationships of love. Let me not cheapen this quality with which you have identified yourself. *Deus caritas est:* if I could only realize this in the handling of that part of me which cries out both for expression and for reciprocated expression I would bring you praise instead of pain. The sense of frustration which accompanies my relationships of affection is only the result of not understanding the implications of your love. The conflict is of my making, not of yours. Lord, let me find peace in the unity of love. Hitherto I have tried to find it either in divine or in human love, but I know that the approach is a mistaken one and can lead to delusion. Teach me now to look to you alone for the solution of my twofold problem, and when I have placed my whole capacity of affection in your hands I shall find myself less divided in my love.

Not until I get to heaven shall I understand this mystery of love. Then will the artificial separation made in the heart and mind of man by original sin give place to truth and unity. In the meantime I must train myself in faith. For the right ordering of his love, a man must have faith and hope. The issue is not so much a psychological and emotional one; it is more a theological and spiritual one. If I can deepen my appreciation of the theological virtues I shall make fewer mistakes in directing my natural desires. While some may come to the knowledge of divine love through the experience of human love, it is more usual that a soul should learn from the love of God how to apply love's principle to the love of other human beings. For this knowledge I pray most earnestly, knowing that without the light of divine wisdom to guide me I shall most certainly deviate into ways which are more of passion than of love. Lord, keep my heart —which is an unquiet member—from straying beyond the boundaries established by Love itself. May your heart be my reference and my ideal.

IT IS A COMMONPLACE to observe that work is a drudgery only if we make it so. We forget that drudgery can be highly sanctifying.

✠ WORK Though we may have chosen the kind of work that suits us best, though we may be interested in it, though we may be conscientious about how we do it, we are not going to escape drudgery. Even the exercise of creative talent, which is supposed to be the most satisfying of all work, must involve drudgery. For any work, however apparently spontaneous, there must be discipline. And discipline means drudgery. But drudgery, we should not forget, is the most salutary of penances and the most humbling of influences. If we could see the virtue which lies in routine labor—see it as Mary and Joseph must have seen it—we would ask for nothing more than to be successful in sweeping, dusting, and washing up.

In itself it is neither the work nor the drudgery that has a disspiriting effect upon us: what exhausts and embitters us is much more often either the hostility which we bring to our work or the wrong sort of energy which we give to it. Work does not drain away our vitality nearly as much as pleasure. Work stimulates our vitality. The man who feels spent, and who wants to retire before his time, is not necessarily the man who has worked himself out. More often the man feels emptied and weary because he has never put anything into the void, has never put his ability to any strain.

Lord, grant that I may not make mistakes about this important aspect of my life. So far as actual time goes, I shall probably be called upon to spend longer hours at my work than at my prayer or at my ease. This is as I want it; I would not have it otherwise. But if so considerable a section of my life is to be taken up in this way, it will need to be directed according to your grace and not according to my impulse. Let me look upon my work as given to me by you. Let me respect it and not merely use it as a means of making money, satisfying an ambition, winning me a reputation. I make the intention of referring it, with all its element of grind on the one hand and all its element of gratification on the other, to you. May you get more glory out of it than I do. May its hardships be united to the hardships which you endured

81

on earth; may its joys take their character from yours.

Spare me, Lord, from being deluded about my work. I know that I am so variable that at one time I am inclined to imagine that none of the work which I do is worth while; at another I am so elated as to imagine that achievement matters more than anything else. At one moment I shall find myself stale with despondency, at another inflated with the idea of success. Faith and humility are my only safeguards. I must believe that the work, however unsatisfactory it seems, is so much material for your greater glory; I must remember too that its outward fruitfulness matters less to you than the dispositions in which it is performed. Lord, I leave to you the task of deciding about fruitfulness; for my part I concern myself with making sure of the disposition. Given your grace I should be able to offer you: first the willingness to go on working as long as I have the strength to do so, next the intention of doing my work as an act of penance and homage, and lastly the readiness to do without the reward of success in this life. Be with me in my work, Lord, and let your Spirit breathe upon it.

CLOSELY CONNECTED with the question of work is the question of vocation. There are three kinds of people whom this subject af-

✠ VOCATION fects: those who feel themselves called to the religious life, those who feel themselves called to life in the world, and those who do not feel themselves called to anything in particular. Of those who think that God may be calling them to live under the vows of religion there are some who are attracted to a particular order or a particular house, while there are others who know only that they want to give themselves more completely to God than they feel they can do if they follow a career in the world. Where, as in the first case, the vocation is more or less clear, the only way to peace is to make a trial of the life. An attraction, however strong, may not guarantee the authenticity of a vocation but at least it is a very strong argument for putting the supposed grace to the test. A man or woman living in the world may not be sure that God is granting the vocation, but the fact that there is an attraction would argue that there might be a vocation to try the vocation.

In the case of those whose call is to a self-dedication of some sort, the form of which is withheld, the immediate duty is to surrender to the Providence of God and to ask for further light. Where the Holy Spirit sees a soul willing to follow his prompting he makes the way clear. He may not make the way clear all at once, but there is nothing to show that a vocation has to be given all at once. Step by step, responding at each stage, the soul comes to know what is the will of God. If we saw the light before we were ready to receive the light we might not follow the light: it is sometimes to our advantage and to the greater glory of God that we do not see—yet.

Among the next group, those who feel nothing of the attraction to the cloister or the mission or the priesthood, there are some who know themselves to be called to matrimony and others to whom the single state seems preferable. Again the course to be followed is that of waiting upon the next grace. Just as it would be idle for the layman whose vocation calls him to live in the world, whether as a married man or not, to envy the vocation of those who are called to the religious life, so it would be idle for the man who is not attracted by marriage to envy the objectively higher vocation of matrimony. Each state carries with it its own graces, and the line for the soul to follow is to make use of what light is granted here and now. If God wants me to raise a family he will provide the circumstances. If he wants me to live on my own and serve him in that way, again he will provide the graces necessary for my perfection in this less usual vocation.

Of the third category, which comprises those unfortunate and foot-loose men and women who nowhere feel at home yet have a true desire to serve God if only he would show them how and where, it must be said that the anchorage now is one of naked faith. It seems almost as if God gives to such souls the vocation to miss their vocation: their sanctity will be found in maintaining their desire to give themselves to God while patiently accepting from him the apparent refusal of their offer. For such souls there will be consolation in the thought of St. Benedict Joseph Labre's vocation. Where there is no vocation either to the religious life, to the priesthood, or to matrimony, there is still the vocation to absolute surrender to God. Lord, give me the grace to make, and mean, the surrender of my whole being to you. This is the first stage in my vocation. If there is more to come, Lord, show me and I will try to be faithful.

WHERE THERE IS DOUBT there can be no true peace or prayer. Whether we doubt a person or a principle, a doctrine or a piece of advice, we are driven back upon ourselves, back upon our insufficiency. ✟ DOUBT It is in our nature to expect a security outside ourselves—either in material affairs or in the return of affection or in God—and if we begin to suspect the security to which our desire is directed we dare not lean any more, we have to rely wholly upon ourselves, we become isolationist and afraid.

The man of many doubts is therefore a man of many miseries: he expects to see flaws in everything and everyone, so he ends by seeing what he wants to see—even if the flaws are not there. The man who fears to count on God's natural creation will be afraid to plant because he doubts the climate, to travel because he doubts the weather, to mix with other men because he doubts his health and theirs. The man who doubts human nature is never at peace because he can never trust anyone's word; he is only waiting to be let down. "I am disillusioned," he says sadly at every reverse — having expected to be. But the man who doubts the Providence of God is the worst off of the three. This man has nothing left. For him there is no security anywhere. To him it seems that the divine attributes have failed to operate in his regard. The danger for such a one is that his doubts should drive him to despair. If doubts drove souls to unbelief it would be bad enough, but almost worse are the doubts which drive—while belief remains—to desperation. There is a return from unbelief but from the extreme of despair there is no return.

Lord, give me the kind of faith which moves the mountains of doubt as well as the molehills of suspicion. Let me cling to the basic virtue of trust: trust in the wisdom which planned the created order, animate and inanimate alike; trust in the truth of revelation, the word itself of Scripture and the power of the Church to interpret Scripture according to the light of your Holy Spirit; trust in your personal concern for me and my affairs.

It is easy enough for me to accept the catechism as it stands. I do not have to hesitate about any of the clauses in the Creed. Dogma upon dogma, definition upon definition: I can take them in my stride knowing that these are not the things which make me wonder. The things that worry me are personal things, Lord, which have to do with grace and free-will and prayer. Lord, show me how to meet my problems in a spirit of unquestioning trust. When I get down to it I seem to know so little about the things which matter most, the three theological virtues. I dare not stake my salvation upon the quality of my love. Yet if I have not love, my faith and hope profit me nothing. Nor do I dare to count upon the steadfastness of my faith. Yet if I doubt, and fail to trust, I no longer love and have nothing to hope for. My hope? Lord, may it be a confident hope, born of love and expressing love, and not a mere wish for what I want. So long as I am in this body I know that my mind will swing this way and that, never perfectly at rest, never enjoying absolute security. Such peace and security are to come. In the meantime I apprehend them in faith. I have no doubts, Lord, or even hesitations. I have only a great longing to be beyond the reach of doubts and hesitations. Lord, help thou my unbelief.

WHILE THERE ARE NO DOUBTS that are good
doubts, except in so far as they occasion contrary
acts of faith, there are certainly fears
✠ FEAR which are good fears. Ecclesiasticus
goes so far as to say that "the fear of
God hath set itself above all things" and again "he
that is without fear cannot be justified." We in
this generation of horror-fiction and neurosis-
literature are perhaps too afraid of fear. We have
to be reminded by Scripture that if we lost all
fear of God, thinking of him only as kindliness
and forgetfulness rather than as justice and truth,
we would lose all grace and virtue. "Unless thou
hold thyself diligently in the fear of the Lord,"
this is again from Ecclesiasticus, "thy house shall
be quickly overthrown." Our alertness in the service of God depends to a large extent upon the
right use of fear. We are always being told that
the life of the Christian is a warfare; it is the fear
of being overcome that keeps us in a state of per-
petual emergency.

Commenting on the verse in the book of Proverbs, "Blessed is the man that is always fearful,"
St. Bernard, who was the most loving and confident
of saints, says this: "I have learned that nothing
is so efficacious in obtaining, keeping, and recover-
ing grace as always to be found fearful before God
and not high-minded. Fear therefore when grace
smiles upon thee, fear when it leaves thee, fear
when it returns again . . . now if grace is restored

88

to thee, thou oughtest much more to fear lest thou suffer a relapse, according to that text of the Gospel which says 'Behold, thou art made whole: sin no more lest some worse thing happen to thee.' "

Lord, in my desire to develop the nobler quality of love I am perhaps too apt to be scornful of fear. I think of it too much as timidity and not enough as the astringent in my service. Remind me from the examples of Samson, Solomon, St. Peter himself, and indeed all the apostles (except St. John), that over-confidence is as much an obstacle as fear. Both fear and false courage spring from lack of faith. It is a curious paradox that we should be living in an age that has reason to fear, and that does indeed fear, but because it has no confidence in God the world is fearing all the wrong things and none of the right ones. The world is moreover placing its confidence, as you would expect it to according to the premise just stated, in all the wrong things and none of the right ones. Just as true fear leads on to true confidence, so false fear leads on to false confidence. "Who art thou that thou shouldst be afraid of a mortal man?" is the ringing challenge of Isaias. Deuteronomy presents the same idea: "Where are their gods in whom they trusted?"

Lord, when you told us to be afraid not of them that have power to kill the body but of them that have power to kill the soul, you gave us the grounds of Christian fear. Higher up the scale we find that our fear must be the dread of offending the Father's love. Higher up again we find that perfect love can cast out fear. Lord, develop my fear for me. I fear the uncertainty of my character in the face of temptation, I fear punishment, I fear offending you. I dare not claim that my love is such that these fears show signs of slackening. But in the end, even if it is not until the next life, I have confidence that all my fears will be swallowed up in the triumph of your love.

THE SUBJECT OF THE LITURGY is best approached objectively, and with no thought at first as to whether or not we feel devotionally attracted to its forms. When the postulates of the liturgy are appreciated, then we can judge of its value to our souls. All too often the liturgy is dismissed from the soul's spiritual horizon because it fails to arouse the emotions in the way that practices of piety are found to do. Only when we have recognized that its primary function is not to rouse the emotions but to satisfy a debt of homage to God are we in a position to talk about the liturgy at all.

✠ **THE LITURGY**

We can take it as an assumed proposition then that there rests upon man, the rational creature made by God and destined to union with God, the obligation of yielding praise and thanksgiving to his Creator. In fulfilling this responsibility man has from the earliest times offered up sacrifices to the Lord, singing before him and performing some sort of ceremonial. The Holy Spirit not only inspired this urge in man but went on to provide the expression to which the urge was to give rise, thus regularizing an articulation that might otherwise have ministered more to self than to God. God wanted himself worshipped in his way rather than in man's way. Man, by worshipping not in his own way but in God's, would be drawn out of himself into God—would find his prayer raised to a new level, would find it given a new value and meaning.

So it is that when we go about our private devotions we give to God an informal and personal homage; when we take part in liturgical worship we are placing our prayer-expression into the text of worship which he himself has framed. In our own prayers we speak naturally and inadequately of God, of our intentions, of ourselves: in liturgical prayer God speaks supernaturally and adequately of himself. "What shalt thou offer to the Lord that is worthy?" asks the prophet Michaeas. "Wherewith shalt thou kneel before the most high God?" And the answer can come from us: "Lord, nothing that *I* am able to offer will be worthy. When I kneel before you there is nothing in *me* that gives due praise. But in reciting the psalms, in taking part in the sacrifice of the Mass, in receiving the sacraments I am echoing your voice, I am sharing in your own prayer as it passes between the Persons of the Trinity, I am caught up into the authentic act of divine love."

Lord, give a great love of your liturgy. Show me that however my mind may wander during the Church's service in which I am taking part, the thread of worship is still there, is going on, is not dependent upon my devotion. Keep my mind attentive so far as possible to the part which I am privileged to play, keep my lips and my movements obedient to the requirements of the chant and ceremonial. When both my mind and my senses are engaged in giving praise to you I am getting back at last to the primary purpose of man. May every faculty of mine—whether intellectual, emotional, or physical—find rest in its proper object which is yourself.

No wonder that the new race of Hebrews can be exhorted: "Let us go therefore with confidence to this throne of grace, that we may obtain mercy and find grace in seasonable aid." Our hope is in the merits of your sacrifice, our prayer is woven into the seamless perfection of your prayer which pays the debt of mankind and brings to the Father's glory its adequate homage.

ARIDITY IN PRAYER is not the same thing as distractions in prayer. A distracted prayer is a nuisance to us because we feel we could ✠ ARIDITY be doing better, and it is humiliating to admit that we have failed. An arid prayer has its distractions like any

92

other but the main problem is not distraction so much as distaste. When we are afflicted with aridity in prayer the disgust can be so great as to send us looking for distraction. So it is not the plague of distractions that humiliates us; what humiliates us is not knowing where we have gone wrong—and not being sure that we mind.

If the aridity has been brought about by laziness, it can be relieved by a more generous response. This is a straightforward issue and presents only the practical difficulty of making the effort. Where on the other hand the aridity is part of the process by which in God's design the soul comes to learn the way of contemplation the difficulty is not that of stirring up energy but of submitting in faith. When the sense of dull impotence has turned into loathing and the search for an excuse to escape the responsibility of the interior life, then it is only faith that can possibly be of any use. Tricks for holding down the attention during prayer-time have ceased to work, meditation-books induce spiritual nausea, devotions which once produced fervor seem now to be insipid, vocal prayer—although it at least guarantees that some kind of prayer activity is going on—has such a routine feel about it that as a means of personal communication it is felt to be inadequate. So what is there but faith? And this is exactly the purpose of the whole painful experience—to force the soul back upon the necessary virtue of faith. Hitherto reliance has been placed upon fervor or method; now the dependence is upon God alone. Hitherto the soul was able to watch the progress and take pleasure in it, to see the industry and take the credit for it; now there is no progress to be seen, and whatever industry is given to the work is felt to be so half-hearted that the less it is looked at the better.

In the matter of aridity there is only one question which we must be able to answer: do I still want to love God in my prayer, going on with the work whatever it costs me, or am I prepared to drop it and think about other ways of serving him? No other question which we can put to ourselves yields any satisfactory answer. If I can say that I want God, I have already found him. If I am willing to put up with the trials of aridity, my prayer is not arid in God's sight but very much the reverse. The aridity that comes from laziness can show no such credentials. The touchstone which distinguishes the true from the false is that of search: if I am searching for God in the darkness of my prayer, if I am sad at not being able to find him and am anxious lest through any fault of mine I have lost his presence, I am on the right way. If I am casual about these things I am not. It is as simple as that—for anyone but the one concerned.

Lord, it looks to me as though the answer to all our problems must in the end be faith. Grant that I may go on believing that these periods of dryness in prayer are what you have planned and not simply what my sins have deserved. Grant that I may have the courage not to complain, not to look for compensations elsewhere, not to force an artificial fervor by flogging my emotions when I should be smothering their demands. I do not ask for relief, Lord, but only for your will.

IF WE ARE ALLOWING religion to do its work in us we should find ourselves becoming increasingly aware of God's presence in his ✠ NATURE works. Where the unbeliever should be able to find his way to belief in God by means of outward creation—St. Paul says that the argument from nature is so strong that they are "inexcusable" who do not proceed from the visible effect to the invisible cause—the believer who is trying to live up to the implications of his faith should be able to see everywhere in the created order symbol after symbol of the divine life. It stands to reason that the deepening of the soul's experience of prayer will lead to the deepening of perception with regard to things outside prayer. Outward things will reflect inward things, and both will be understood in terms of the one reality. If prayer and faith are the means by which a soul draws close to God and comes to a loving knowledge of truth, prayer and faith are also the means by which a soul comes to a true knowledge and appreciation of God's works. In their turn, knowledge and appreciation of God's

95

works contribute to the soul's interior operation of love.

Thus for a man of prayer to dismiss the whole subject of created beauty as of only secondary importance when the main interest is the love and service of God would be to leave out of account a significant medium of divine revelation. It would also betray the fact that there was a flaw somewhere in the man's prayer — the prayer having failed in one of its more necessary consequences.

Nor is it only in the work of nature that man should see the reflected light of God. He should see it in the work of man's hands as well as in the work of God's. Human intelligence is the gift of God, and the fruit of human intelligence is just as much the gift of God as the fruit which comes out of the earth or which hangs upon a tree. A scientific discovery comes to us, at one remove or many, from God. This is not to say that all fruit is good fruit, and that every piece of machinery is a good piece of machinery. There are fruits of wickedness and there are material things which are constructed by men for evil. But in all this the man of prayer can see a symbol of the spiritual, can see the conflict between Lucifer and Michael.

Lord, I pray that I may see. I pray that my appreciation of nature, of physical beauty, of human intelligence, of works of art, of science and of every study may deepen my love of you and show me new facets of your splendor. Until I am admitted to the state of the blessed in heaven I shall always have to look for you in signs and symbols, always you will speak to me from behind a veil; let me read the signs in faith and in faith penetrate the veil. With the act of creation came the justification of creatures; let me not presume to despise them. You who pronounced creation to be good can give me the grace of seeing it always so. The objects that present themselves to my senses are so many rungs in the ladder by which I mount to you; let me use them as such and not attempt to fly. Grant that the world may learn from your revelation, from Scripture and from the right use of the forms which you have chosen in the expression of your mind to man, to come back to you instead of allowing these very forms to separate you from your own.

FOR THE MAN who is trying to live his Christianity to the full, for the man of prayer, art is nothing but the revelation of the truth and ✠ ART beauty of God. Whether he is himself an artist or not, the Christian has a responsibility towards the Christian conception of art. He may not evade the issues to which the Christian aesthetic gives rise. He may not say that he is not interested in the subject, or, with a flourish of modesty, that he is not qualified to judge. Art is a thing about which we have to make up our minds. This is not to say that we have to study the principles of this and that branch of art, that we have to possess canons of judgment or be ready with arguments with which to justify our taste. Still less does it mean that in taking the religious view of art we must want to make all art specifically religious, or that our powers of appreciation refuse to look beyond the one field which is religious. If such were the demand to be made of those who have chosen to follow the way of grace, the artistic judgment of every religious person would have to be the same, and would be made for him.

In so far as its purpose is to reveal an aspect of beauty, all art can be thought of as religious art. An artist may be clumsy, may be muddle-headed in his theory, may be a bad man in his private life, may have as his motive for working at his medium either publicity, money, personal satisfaction in the exercise of a talent, desire to go one better than his rivals in the same line, but so long as he is trying to produce an object which is true and beautiful he is bearing witness to the truth and beauty of God. He may be unconscious of this testimony which his work brings, he may even not want to bring it, he may seek to profane the God whom he knows or seek to escape from the God whom he does not want to know, but the work of his hands which he has made goes beyond his own creative powers to his Creator's. The work itself may be hideous, but this does not alter the fact that it could not come into being at all but for two things, both of them essentially related to beauty: first, the fact that it reflects something thought of in the mind of the artist as either beautiful or true—as something worth producing; second, the fact that God gave to the artist the ability to produce it—God himself being beautiful and true.

Lord, when the amateur steps into the world of professional art he is likely to expose himself to humiliation and bewilderment. Without wanting to complicate my direct approach to you with controversy about the indirect approaches to you, I do want to learn more of truth and beauty than what I can learn from a theological text-book: I want to see divine truth underlying artistic truth, divine beauty as the prototype of artistic beauty. Not in the visual arts alone, but in music, literature, the drama and the ballet—in every expression of human talent—let me look for your inspiration. In the whole range of human achievement throughout the centuries of history I should be able to trace your guiding finger. The design is yours, the material is yours, and the inspiration and end are yours. The instrument, man, is also yours. I pray that these human instruments which we call artists may come more and more to recognize their role on earth and may acquit themselves of the responsibility to which their talents render them liable. May they arrive, as I pray that I may also, at the understanding of creatures in relation to the Creator.

FEW CAN CLAIM to be such independent thinkers that they can remain uninfluenced by what they read. While our opinions may

✠ READING not be shaped by the press, while our tastes may not be developed by our choice of reading, papers and books have nevertheless a power of direction which we perhaps recognize only when we start recommending literature to those in whose cultural or spiritual welfare we are interested.

When our Lord told his followers "he that hath ears to hear, let him hear," he might equally have said "he that hath eyes to see, let him read." When St. Paul said that "faith cometh by hearing," he meant that there had to be some external channel through which the grace might be conveyed. Faith comes also by reading. The word is the same whether spoken or written. "The word that goeth forth from the mouth of God," as Isaias says, "must not return to him void." In a sense it cannot go back to him void: it is either believed and loved or denied and ignored. For good or ill there is a contribution of some sort.

Man may not live apart from God's word, may not silence it or so multiply his own words as not to hear it, may not go to the world in search of a noise loud enough to drown the voice of God. When a man cuts himself off from the voice of God he cuts himself off from life. His soul, insulated from the sound that is life-giving, dies. "Not by bread alone does man live," it is written in Deuteronomy, and so important is the statement that Christ himself quotes it when he is tempted on the mountain, "but by every word that proceedeth from the mouth of God." The word of God gives life, and the Word of God made flesh gives perfect life. At the word of the Father the world came into being; at the word of the Son it was redeemed. And the final dissolution of the world must wait upon the word of God.

Not only does the word give life but when that life is weakened it brings health. "Say but the word and my soul shall be healed." My soul must listen for the word, must be made familiar with its accent and expression. How can this familiarity be developed if the recorded words of God are never read? If, when read, they are explained away? If I am to know the word, still more if I am to echo it in my prayer and conduct, I must do two things: I must approach written revelation with a mind receptive to the meaning which it has for my soul, and I must control my secular reading.

Lord God, I pray that your Holy Spirit may guide me in my study and in my recreation, in what I choose to read and in what I refuse to read. I pray for the light by which I shall know what is meant, and by which I shall benefit from what I understand. I pray for the presence of mind which will warn me immediately of material that is dangerous, and for the courage to act upon such prompting. I pray that the concessions which others allow in their reading may not set the standard for me: the only authority which has a right to set the standard of my reading is your own. Through my prayer and through my conscience, Lord, suggest to me the course to follow. In this matter of reading I need to learn from you, and not from my friends, the measure best suited to my soul and to the glory of your name.

"SINS, BE THEY LITTLE OR GREAT," says St. Augustine, "cannot go unpunished; whence the Lord enjoined David to do penance

✠ PENANCE for his sin in numbering the people that he should either suffer seven years' famine, three months' vengeance from his enemies, or three days' pestilence. And David chose for himself and his people the common scourge of death. By this is signified that everyone shall certainly be punished for his sins either in hell or in purgatory or by some present affliction." The soul cannot come to God except by the way of innocence, or, when this is lost, by the way of penitence. In the third chapter of St. Matthew we find St. John the Baptist preaching the necessity of penance, and if this is not enough to convince us, we have in St. Matthew's fourth chapter the account of how Christ himself opened his mission with the same doctrine. In St. Luke we find the same theme from our Lord's lips: "Except you do penance, you shall all perish." We moderns are inclined to think and talk as though penance were a virtue insisted upon by the prophets of the Old Testament but which has been superseded in the New Testament by a better understanding of mercy and love. Earlier generations of Christians did not feel this. *Aut penitendum,* growls quite correctly a certain old father of the desert, *aut ardendum.* Those rougher ages, nearer to Christ in point of time, were in many things nearer to Christ in thought and practice. No sooner had the Bridegroom left them than the wedding guests showed their love by exchanging the wedding garment for the dress of penance. We, coming later in history, have inherited in this matter a weakened tradition.

It is no good pretending to hate our sins while refusing to do penance for them. It is no good praying with compunction about the weakness of our corrupt flesh if we make little attempt to mortify the senses which stir up the evils in our corrupt flesh. It is no good weeping compassionate tears in our consideration of Christ's Passion if we refuse to allow Christ's Passion to reproduce itself at any point in our lives.

As to the practical side of penance—how we are to go about it—we get sound advice from St. Albert the Great where he says that "as particular infirmities of the body have their appropriate medicines, so special sins have their special penance. Pride is not directly cured by giving alms, nor envy by prayer, nor avarice by fasting . . . but we satisfy for pride by humility, for avarice by giving alms, for impurity by chastisement of the flesh, for gluttony by fasting, for talkativeness by silence, for envy by charity, and so on." But since we cannot realize the whole debt of satisfaction we must also offer, together with the token offerings of our penitence of heart, the Son's infinite merits in adequate atonement to the Father.

Lord, here then is my cue. I do what I can in the way of showing, by concrete acts of mortification, that I am sorry for my sins. But I know that these do not carry me all the way. Indeed they are so insignificant that they carry me hardly any way at all. But it is not in my acts of penance that I put my trust: I trust in your Passion to provide me with all that is needed to satisfy the Father's justice. Left to themselves my penances are useless, but referred to you through the sufferings of Calvary they acquire a value out of all proportion to their intrinsic worth. In union with the sacrifice of Calvary, the sacrifice of the Mass, I offer my oblation in penitence of heart.

St. Gregory says that it is by three degrees or stages that we are introduced to the grace of that true interior prayer which

✠ RECOLLECTION is contemplation: by recollection, by meditation, by cogitation. "The first," he says, "is that the soul recollect itself to itself. The second is that it should see itself as its recollection reveals. The

104

third is that it should rise above itself, attending to the contemplation of God." It is the first point that concerns us here, and about this St. Gregory goes on to say: "The soul can by no means recollect itself unless it has first learned to reject the images of earthly and even heavenly things from the eye of the mind . . . all those things are to be driven away from the mind by the hand of discretion so that the soul may be able to consider itself as it is under God." This is the recollection which is proposed every time the soul sets about the work of addressing God in prayer.

But there is another recollection which the soul must try to acquire—a recollection which directly promotes the exercise mentioned by St. Gregory and which is to a large extent assumed by it. This is the more general recollection practiced outside the set periods of prayer. It consists in the attempt to live so far as possible in the presence of God. The habit of recollection, as distinct from the act of recollection as performed in prayer, is something which many could enjoy if they set themselves to persevere in responding to its attraction. The grace is there; all that is needed is the generosity to return again and again to the thought of God. The soul "re-collects" the thoughts of God which previous prayer has engendered and which earthly affairs have subsequently obscured. The soul "re-collects" its own interior faculties and directs them towards their proper object, namely God. The soul "re-collects" its perceptions which have become scattered among the distractions of ordinary outward life, and allows the presence of God to occupy the whole horizon. When this habit is acquired in its perfection it amounts to the grace of contemplation itself—the grace which gathers together all the effective and rational powers of the soul so that the divine nature is known and loved. "It is good for me," confesses the Psalmist, "to cleave to my God." *Adhaerere* is the word used, the implication is that the soul sticks constantly to God. It means more than remaining faithful; it means remaining close. How else than by recollection?

Lord, grant me the attraction for this kind of prayer. I know that it is a grace which can open up vistas of the interior life, and of the possibilities of religion, which will make my service a living and a loving reality. Recollection should be able to turn the waste spaces of my day into periods of fruitful supernatural activity. Let me not complain that there are no waste spaces which can be turned in this way, and that I have no time in the kind of busy life I lead to give to recollection: I know that the grace of habitual prayer has nothing to do with time but has everything to do with response. Let me respond to the first movements of recollection, Lord, and from that stage onwards I can trust that you will give me the light to know what to do next. Again with the Psalmist I can say—this time to my own soul—the verse: "Turn, O my soul, into thy rest; for the Lord hath been bountiful to thee." My recollection is at once your praise and my most secure rest. Lord, admit me to the peace of soul which is recollection.

ON THIS SUBJECT the ideal is suggested in the fourth chapter of the Acts of the Apostles where

✠ **SOCIAL OBLIGATION** we are told that in the primitive Church "the multitude of believers had but one heart and one soul." Here was social unity in its perfection. The heart and soul were Christ's. Christ's spirit, operating among his faithful, calls forth from the human soul a reflection of the divine activity. "Nothing is more worthy," says St. John Chrysostom, "than that a man be an imitator of his Creator, and execute the divine work according to the measure of his own faculties." Living in concord with God, we must live in concord with men. If God works among men in charity, sharing his life with them, man has the obligation of reproducing this same work. This is the whole principle of social obligation—that we do as God does, and do it for his sake.

But it is easy for us to deceive ourselves in matters connected with charity. We can persuade ourselves that we are satisfying our social obligation in charity when in fact we are satisfying only social conventions. The negative tests are sometimes more revealing in this context than those which relate to what we do positively. We may behave with positive good manners, but unless we back this up with equally positive good-will we are no more than good-behaviorists. Our social responsibility is being neglected, then, if our aim is to impose our own will on the community, to draw the opinions of others to our own way of thinking, to demand attention, to attract affection—especially when this means attracting some people's affection away from those to whom it has already been given—and in general to assert our own rights at the expense of everyone else's. A clear sign that we have got the wrong idea of our responsibility is that we resent the evidence of it in those whose charity is a standing witness to its presence in them and to its absence in us.

Lord, I pray that your charity may so manifest itself in me that my uncharitable disposition may be no obstacle to its exercise. Let me come to see my place not only in your mystical body but also in the particular social body to which I belong. Grant that I may not, either by laziness, thoughtlessness, intolerance or consideration of class or money, exclude anyone from the range of my hospitality. Grant also that in the exercise of those duties which the world would regard as purely social—the entertaining of friends, repaying debts of kindness, taking part in bazaars and so on—I may propose to myself a strictly charitable, and therefore a supernatural, purpose. Let nothing be wasted, nothing be spent in the way either of energy or time or money, on enterprises which do not have you as their final object. Lord, I see so much in the way of benevolence all around me, and I find myself constantly in admiration of people's generosity: draw the good material towards yourself, Lord, and reward the souls of these kind hosts and benefactors with the grace of seeing deeper into the essential act of giving.

If it is your will that man should not save his soul alone, without reference to the salvation of others, it must consequently be your will that each of us owes obligations beyond that of rendering necessary assistance when called upon in a crisis. I must, as you did, go out of my way to save. I cannot guarantee to save, but at least I can guarantee to help. Lord, launch me on this project, and give it your blessing.

WE FIND OUR SANCTIFICATION not in triumphing over our lot in life but in living according to it as

 FAMILY OBLIGATION God designed it for us. Once we know what our setting is, we do not have to break out of it in order to find the means to high sanctity: we find within it the appropriate means to sanctity. Moreover if the means thus provided are not directed to God they will be directed away from God and will provide means of destruction. In the spiritual order nothing can remain neutral. We live on a ladder, and are forever going up or going down; there is no sitting on the ladder and waiting for the rungs to move in an upward direction. So if marriage is my God-given vocation it will be through marriage and not in spite of it that I shall become a saint. If I am called by God to work as a lawyer it will be the law that either sanctifies me or condemns me. A schoolmaster finds either help or hindrance in his teaching; the missioner finds only temptation in his apostolic work where he does not find in it the means to spread the Gospel and sanctify his own soul. To a member of a family the graces of a family-vocation are given, and if these are neglected there is not only waste but serious danger of sin.

"There is not a state in the world that has not its bitterness and crosses," says St. Vincent de Paul, "and which therefore does not make us desire some other condition. Our perfection consists in uniting our will with that of God in such a manner as to will only what he wills." Our whole duty then is to re-live the Christ-life within the framework of the life which is given us.

Just as a religious house is a unit which has to be maintained by the combined effort of its members, so the human family demands a corresponding contribution from those who make up its number. The responsibility extends beyond material considerations, demanding loyalty and mutual trust among the members. Where there is an atmosphere of mistrust, there will be furtive infidelities. Where love is lacking in the household, love will be looked for elsewhere. Where the joys of family life are made to consist in artificial enjoyments, the true satisfaction proper to the state is no longer felt to be attractive. The household, like a monastery, is a single thing and has a corporate activity. Unless the life is shared—which means holding in common a variety of elements such as work, sorrows, secrets, hopes and ambitions, joys, and, above all, religious practice and aspiration — there is bound to be a want of balance. The happiest families are those where the members have the same conscience about spiritual and moral matters, the same outlook in matters intellectual and recreative.

Lord, let me see in the natural family what monks and nuns are trained to see in their supernatural families. The vows are different but the bond must be the same—namely charity. And just as religious houses are always in danger of losing their true spirit by reason of pressures which threaten from without, so I must know that the same pressures are liable to threaten the inward strength of the family. Where I find myself sacrificing my family obligations to economic, political, business or sporting interests, I must know that I am tampering with the order of things. Lord, give me a sense of due perspective which will enable me to be faithful both to my family and to you. In perfecting this fidelity I shall at the same time perfect my own vocation.

THE PRINCIPLE OF JUSTICE is as clear and uncompromising as a mountain; where we go wrong is

✠ BUSINESS OBLIGATION

in the interpretation and the refinements. By looking through the wrong end of the telescope we can reduce the mountain to a molehill, and there is nothing easier than stepping over molehills. The first thing to remember is that denying to men what is just in business is denying to God what is just in worship. "The just shall rejoice in the Lord," says the Sixty-third Psalm, "and shall hope in him." We have no right to hope in the Lord unless we are just in our dealings with men. Yet we are all too familiar with instances of that dichotomy which allows a business man to present himself before God in the church as a Christian without reproach while presenting himself before a board-meeting as a tycoon who would be ready to go in for any sharp practice which would bring off a deal.

The excuse is always that in business no one is above a little dishonesty, and that in order to get on one must make use of the recognized technique. "Even in order to safeguard one's interests, let alone make money, one cannot afford to take the Sermon on the Mount too literally. The Sermon on the Mount simply would not work today. If others were as honest as I want to be, all would be well; but while keeping a love for honesty and justice in my heart, I find myself regretfully compelled to forget these noble qualities when doing business." Man who is the finest product of the Creator's hand, who has been raised by Wisdom itself to be lord of the universe, possesses, as Chesterton somewhere observes, this one defect — he cannot be trusted. The untrustworthy nature of one man elicits what is untrustworthy in another. And so it goes on until no one trusts anyone else.

But let us get to the heart of this matter. Justice was not invented for the purpose of securing equity in trade negotiations. Nor is it simply a means of insurance against exploitation, aggression, political or national domination. Why is a man called upon to be just? Why is it unjust to take away a man's name by slander or a man's wife by seduction? Why is unfairness, whether in business or education or international relations, an affront against the created order? The answer can be put in a verse from the Tenth Psalm: "The Lord is just and hath loved justice." We are made in the image and likeness of God. He is our pattern, he is also our justice. Dishonesty is not simply a sin against another man; it is a sin against the conception of man. It is not simply the transgression of a law; it is the violation of a purpose. It is not simply the destruction of something outside the man who is guilty of it; it is the destruction of something inside him—it is the destruction of his resemblance to Christ.

"The just shall rejoice in the Lord . . . rejoice in the Lord, all ye just . . . let no injustice have dominion over me." Why all this emphasis on justice? Is not charity more important? This is perhaps where our mistake lies—that we separate the two. But charity is justice, and justice is charity. Charity is not something which begins where justice leaves off; justice is not an elementary form of charity suitable for beginners. Unless justice is informed by charity and itself expresses charity it can confine itself to the law-courts. Our justice is from God and must be referred back to God. Lord, in the light of divine love show me the inwardness of justice.

WE KNOW FROM ST. JAMES what constitutes true religion: works of charity and the renunciation of

 RELIGIOUS OBLIGATION

the world. St. Peter amplifies this by saying that the religious man "flees carnal desires which war against the soul." From here we can turn to St. Augustine, who further elaborates the idea where he says that "he lives according to the flesh who lives according to himself. He goes where he will; sleeps when he will and as long as he will; speaks what he will, to whom he will, and where he will; eats and drinks when he will and as much as he will; laughs and takes base pleasure amongst whom

114

he will . . . because he carnally wills all things lawful and unlawful." While the earlier sentences of this quotation give us the picture of the worldling, the concluding sentence gives us the summing up of worldliness: irreligion is not only willing what is contrary to religion but is just as significantly willing carnally what happens to be within religion's legitimate compass. Just as the essence of religion is turning the will away from the world and directing it towards God, so the essence of irreligion is the claim to that independence of God which allows a man to turn his will in any direction he pleases. The truly irreligious man is "given over to a reprobate sense" whereby he judges those things to be lawful to him which are not, and even those things which are lawful he desires in a way which is not.

From the above it can be deduced that our responsibility as men and women pledged to the service of religion—the word "religion" being understood here in the wider sense and not as referring to the religious life—is the responsibility of remaining "as pilgrims and strangers" in the world. We must "use this world as though we used it not"; we must share with our ancestors of the Old Testament the sense of homesickness for the city of God. If we are in all things identical with our pagan neighbors—one with them in our moral standards, our views on current subjects, our amusements, ambitions and taboos—we are irreligious people. If the only difference between me and my non-Catholic friends is to be found in my choice of fish on one day of the week and the half hour that I spend at Mass every Sunday, then it looks as though I am taking my religious obligation very much too lightly. Certainly I am not living by faith, I am not making the Gospel life my own, I am not taking my stand on the life of Christ.

Lord, grant me a lively sense of my Catholic inheritance. Let me not cheapen the good thing which through no merit of mine I have been privileged to enjoy. Prevent me from adjusting myself to the prevailing unbelief, to the outlook which puts expedience before principle and human well-being before everything else. Give me a Catholic conscience which will enable me to judge, in those borderline cases which are bound to come up in social life, what is your will. Do not allow me always to take the lax view in questions of abstinence, the Sunday obligation, the practice of Lent and other religious observances. Give me the courage which will enable me to present the Catholic case to non-Catholics, and to defend its claims. Remind me that it is part of my religious obligation to know what the Church teaches, and also, by word and example, to expound that teaching. Since my most precious possession in this world is my faith, I pray that I may cherish and not endanger it.

SCRIPTURE TELLS US that our lives are worth more in God's sight than the lives of sparrows, that the hairs of our heads are numbered, and that we may confidently rely upon divine providence to provide us with what is necessary. Why then do we worry about whether we shall be well enough for this or that, whether we dare risk going out in the wet, whether we ought not to go to bed in case we get worse? We should remember that the Scripture further tells us that "all things work together for our good." If this means anything it must mean that in the question of health we are always in the condition best suited to what God wants of us here and now. This does not mean that we are free to be reckless on the one hand, or so cautious in preserving exactly that condition on the other that we do not stir for fear of exposing ourselves to infection. It means that the less we think about health the better.

✟ HEALTH

The human body is a good thing; it comes from God. But it is not such a good thing that everything else has to defer to its well-being. Money is a good thing, wine is a good thing, flowers and dogs and goldfish are good things; but these good things must not be allowed to dominate. Nor may they be hoarded. We can hoard the good of health as a miser hoards money; we can indulge our taste for health as a drunkard indulges his taste for drink. We can make a fetish of health as people will make a fetish of pets. Of all manias, the health mania is perhaps the most unhealthy.

Considering how easy it is to apply the tests, and what clear findings result, it is strange that we are so readily deceived about the importance of health. Where we go wrong is in thinking of health as a thing on its own, as a thing worth making a fuss about because it is a nice thing to have and because it obviously comes as a gift from God. The satisfaction it brings is a legitimate satisfaction. But if we would handle the question right we ought not to look upon it as a non-sinful luxury to be exhibited but as a means of rendering greater glory to God. In other words health is always to be seen in relation to the will of God. Since God's will is signified in the circumstances which surround our lives, health is to be referred through circumstances to God. Thus health is emphatically not a good on its own, an end: it is a relative good, and must always be viewed in relation to other goods. Experience will reveal how often, if this course is followed, the importance of health will have to yield to the far greater importance of other things.

Lord, shield me from the wailings of an ill-conceived attitude towards health. If I give in to the pleadings, warnings, arguments, scoldings which come to me from a pampered body I shall end by being a crank. Let not considerations of health have the final word in anything whatever. The primary question is your holy will, and if I judge that a certain course to follow is the course which you want me to follow, I must overrule the excuse of health. I know that I have nothing to fear if I trust in you. Your strength is my strength; I do not put my confidence in the powers of a robust body any more than I put my trust in the powers of a determined character. If I cannot, by taking thought, add to my natural stature, neither can I, by taking precautions which limit my service of religion, add to my stature in your sight.

THE DANGER of becoming money-minded is every bit as great as the danger of becoming health-minded. Radically they arise from

✠ MONEY the same lack of faith, from the same preoccupation with the material side of life, from the same kind of selfishness which takes personal convenience and well-being to be more important than anything else in the world. Both evils offend constantly against charity, patience, detachment and self-control.

Leaving aside the call to voluntary poverty which is a specific aspect of this question, there is for all followers of Christ the more general call to the regulation of money according to right reason. Wanton extravagance, for example, is a sin on any showing. Ostentation is a sin of pride whether or not it can be afforded. The man, moreover, who is so eager to accumulate wealth that he will not consider the needs of others, is sinning against justice as well as against charity. The predominant

119

sin of the miser is greed, but greed never stops short at itself. Thus it may be said that love of money draws away the soul from the virtues and replaces them with vices. And if even the philosophers who had no knowledge of God renounced wealth because of the independence which such a renunciation gave them, it must surely be part of the Christian philosophy to renounce superfluity for more strictly religious reasons.

The world is feverish in its greeds, is torn by material anxiety, is restless in everlasting competition. Christ counters all this when he says that we must take no thought for the morrow, must keep calm in the knowledge that God does not forget about the creatures which he has made, must avoid making the mistake of the rich man Lazarus. To illustrate his doctrine further, he gives us the alarming illustration of the camel and the needle's eye. But even if he had said nothing at all about the danger of riches and the blessedness of an accepted poverty, Christ would have preached the gospel of detachment from material things by his life and death. "In the left hand of God were riches and glory," says St. Bernard in his sermon for Christmas Eve, "and in his right hand length of life. Of all these things there was an eternal abundance in heaven, but poverty was not found there. On earth, however, poverty did abound and superabound; and man knew not its value. Wherefore God, being enamoured of it, came down that he might make choice of it for himself, and that he might also, by his esteem of it, make it precious to us."

Lord, even though I may not be able to rise to the challenge of voluntary poverty I can at least forswear covetousness. I will try by your grace to endure what privations I may have to suffer, and not to cry out in complaint. I will try not to allow anxiety about the future weigh with me, knowing that financial security is not as important as it seems. But in telling you here of the things which I mean to do in preserving detachment of heart I am touching only the fringe of the matter: what counts much more is what you will do in me. Teach me where my real security lies. Grant that my treasure may really be in heaven and not where the rust and the moth can get at it. If by your help I can place my whole happiness in serving you, I shall not bother about the spurious happiness which, as the world imagines, may be found in earthly possessions. From your cross, Lord, teach me the ideal of Christian detachment.

IF IT IS WORLDLY to think in terms of money, it is no less worldly to think in terms of class. In fact a man is more truly worldly who ✚ CLASS bases his judgments on considerations of social than of financial status: the worldliness is not now the superficial worldliness of vulgarity but the more subtle worldliness of superiority. Few people attach any moral worth to the possession of money whereas many would see virtue in the possession of ancestry. Breeding and upbringing have their value; so also have wealth and property. But so far as moral worth goes, these things are accidental: they can be of unlimited value to the man who seeks first the kingdom of heaven; they can be a very great obstacle to the kingdom of heaven to the man who puts them first.

What, to make a list, are those benefits which can come to a man through the tradition which he inherits from his father? Culture, good manners, respect for order and authority and the past, a certain way of talking, control of the emotions in public, loyalty to the caste or clan. These are qualities eminently worth having. But they do not entitle their possessors to superiority. They are not the prerogative of a single class. They are not passports to eternal life. Like every gift of nature or grace, the gift which comes to us by way of our parents is one for which we should be grateful to God. We show our gratitude by using it as he wants it to be used, by referring it, directly or indirectly, back again to him. There is this also to be noted, that where these inherited advantages are irresponsibly enjoyed the guilt is greater than in the case of irresponsibility lower down the social scale. Of those to whom much is given, much is required again. God does not shower favors upon one class rather than upon another, and then decide to overlook the question of stewardship. Whether his gift takes the form of money, health, brain or breeding, the parable of the talents points to the kind of account which will be demanded.

In telling us that the kingdom of heaven is not in meat and drink, Lord, you surely meant us to conclude that it was not in accent and mannerism either. Help me to rise above shibboleths of class, so that I think no worse of a person because he pronounces words in a certain way, uses the wrong terms, is ignorant of conventions which are recognized by the older families. Nor let my inbred snobbishness be the influence which allows me to see the finer qualities of those who happen to have been born in higher walks of life. I am grateful for the background and education which your divine providence has arranged for me; I do not envy, nor do I despise, these things where I see them possessed at a different level by others. If a deepening of my spirit of faith gives me the solution to the problem of wealth, the same will solve my difficulties regarding class. It is idle, as well as unsupernatural, to look for an even distribution of God's gifts among men. I accept the distribution as it is, knowing that those who are less well educated, less comfortably off, less blessed with either lineage or looks, will enjoy compensating graces. Whom do you commend in Gospel, Lord, when you come to the reckoning? The intelligent, the powerful, the rich and aristocratic? No, but rather the obscure: "because thou hast been faithful in a *few* things" — which were all the man had — "therefore I will place thee over many."

THE MIGRATORY STIRRING which seems to be such a psychological feature of our age is a manifestation which calls for control on the part of souls who are proposing to follow the spiritual life. Even if it does not constitute a threat to perseverance, it makes steadfastness very difficult. "All change delights the heart," wrote Seneca in a hopeful mood, but there is a danger in pursuing a delight which demands frequent repetition. Washington Irving develops Seneca's observation where he says that there is relief in change "even though it be for the worse." We can become like people suffering from a fever, constantly turning over and finding themselves each time in a more uncomfortable position.

✠ RESTLESSNESS

To feel the desire for change is morally neither good nor bad. It is the same, ethically, as to feel the desire for sleep or food. But like so many other desires that are not forbidden as being wrong, the desire for change leads to consequences which are only in exceptional cases right. To break out of the existing environment—if it has once been recognized as the environment created for the soul by God—requires a reason stronger than restlessness. Restlessness, moreover, can masquerade as legitimate ambition, as desire to escape occasions of sin,

124

as zeal in spreading the spirit of the Gospel over a wider field. Still admitting that change *may* be a good thing, even a *necessary* thing, the claim made here is that its motives must be watched.

Why do we want to alter the frame in which God has set us? Is it not often because we lack the patience to wait until he alters it for us? Is it not because we trust our own judgment, thinking that we know better than God what is good for us? Is it not greed for happiness—our own kind of happiness which we feel we may miss if we delay any longer? Are we not afraid that if we stay on as we are we shall find life getting harder instead of easier?

"I do not despair of happier times," says St. John Chrysostom in an illuminating passage of self-revelation, "knowing well that God is at the helm of the universe and that he overcomes the storm not by skill but by his *fiat*. I know that he does not do so all at once, and that if a change for the better is despaired of by the many he nevertheless manifests his marvelous work. In acting thus he exercises his prerogative and at the same time tries the endurance of his faithful afflicted. Never be cast down, then, for one thing alone is to be feared, namely sin."

Lord, enlighten me in those situations which call for the decision to move or to stay. Let me be able to distinguish between the impulse of grace and the motive of selfishness. I want only to do what

125

pleases you, and if I act in a hurry I shall almost certainly please myself. To please myself while displeasing you will lead me in the end to pleasing nobody. Grant that I may take as objective a view as possible, seeing the occasion first as related to your will, then as related to the happiness of others, and only when I have been able to satisfy myself on those two points let me take into consideration my private leanings in the matter. Lord, give me a love of single-mindedness and steadfastness. Let me not be at the mercy of whims. I cannot follow all vocations; let me be careful and constant in following the one which you have given to me.

PEOPLE WHO WOULD NOT DREAM of misusing property, their own or belonging to others, are often reckless in the misuse of time—their **✝ TIME** own and other people's. It is not only the things that can be seen that are material: time is a material gift from God like any other in the created order and must be treated as such. If time were a solid which we could watch evaporating as we wasted it, it would be valued more; its invisibility is its handicap—its reproaches are veiled.

If we could understand the value of time, seeing it in relation to eternity, we would rate it higher than even health or natural beauty. In the span of half a minute a man may lose or save his soul. No earthly goods can claim to be the medium of so extreme a contrast. By the right use of time when no crisis is going on a man prepares himself for the time of emergency. If his mind is flabby from the habitual waste of time it will delay his decision: he will play for time, and there will not be enough of it. Spiritual writers of the old school were at pains to show how a sinner on his deathbed would give anything to reclaim his wasted hours but would be at a loss to know how profitably to employ this, his last, hour. It is perhaps a pity that we who pride ourselves upon an unsentimental approach to the deathbed scene should be scornful of this idea about time. Trite as it may be to say that time cannot be reclaimed, it is precisely this that gives such significance to everything that we do during it. All our acts in this life are framed in time. At death our works will be taken out of one frame and put into another.

But it is not only for our own sake that we must come to an agreement with time; more importantly it is for God's sake. He is the giver of time, and in justice to him we have to spend it as he wants it spent. A servant would fail in justice who treated his employer's goods with carelessness or contempt. Though we may not be particularly tempted to despise time, we nevertheless act as if we did. We seek to kill time, we let hours of it slip through our fingers, we discover that days have gone by and we have not the least recollection of how we spent them, we would be hard put to it to give an account of the constructive work that we had done in our

127

time. We talk glibly about "free" time and "my own time" and "time off," but even time for recreation is a space to be used: recreation time is not a void that can be left a void. Blank spaces are blank only in preparation. We shall not be required at the judgment to produce empty pages which can be accounted for only in terms of the harm which they might have recorded; their emptiness is harm enough.

Lord, you have bought us this gift of time with the use which you made of the time that you spent on earth. Am I going to waste both the gift and the price which you paid? My time belongs more to you than it does to me, so help me to do justice to its opportunity. I know that the right use of time does not mean the strained use of time, does not demand intense application of mind and body at every moment of the waking day, but I know too that there must be discipline in the way that it is spent. Without either laziness on the one hand, or scruple on the other, I want so to occupy the time you have lent me that it may bring glory to your name and fit me for an eternity where no moment will be wasted or misused.

JUST AS TIME is not given to man for himself alone, so neither is the power of speech. A man may not speak solely for his own

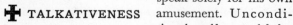 **✠ TALKATIVENESS** amusement. Unconditional talk would be more of a menace to society than unconditional

128

time. Carried beyond a certain point the use of speech is a waste of itself and a waste of time. Accordingly if we want to use the faculty of speech as it is meant by God to be used, we must examine the conditions attaching to it. The first and most obvious qualifications are that we speak what is true, what is constructive, what is to the glory of God. St. Paul urges us to echo in our conversation the psalms, hymns, and spiritual canticles which directly gave praise to God. Our conversation, further, must be "upright before God," and the evils which men commit may not be mentioned among us as topics of scandal and idle gossip. No lying or filthy speech, for we take our standard from the saints. St. James makes great point about the necessity of keeping the faculty of speech directed in a single course: the division comes, he says, when we use the faculty at one moment in giving praise to God and at the next in tearing our neighbor to pieces. The fountain must send up a single jet of water, not half of it bitter and half of it sweet.

But the conditions are more far-reaching than this. It is a question not only of matter but of manner. Souls who have examined their consciences and resolved with great earnestness to avoid all topics which are remotely connected with evil may yet sin against the use of speech by talking of suitable things unsuitably. Though a man may talk about God he will not please God if he talks when he is meant to keep silent. A man may be moved

129

by the excellent motive of charity to speak to his neighbor, but if he speaks too much he wearies his neighbor and charity is not served. The speaker must always bear in mind that by talking immoderately, thoughtlessly, out of turn, in a way which prevents anyone else talking, and about things which may be harmless enough to him and interesting enough to him but which carry no guarantee that they are the same to others, he may be an occasion of sin to his audience.

Among spiritually minded people the evil of effusiveness in spiritual matters is much to be guarded against. The harm is not in the spiritual subjects discussed but in the effusiveness with which they are discussed. Behind the desire to bare the soul to another there may often be vainglory and the purely natural longing to talk about oneself. There is a danger also that in these spiritual colloquies the emotions may get carried away, and that the grace of true spirituality will be dissipated by such outpourings. The truly interior soul is reluctant to discourse on what grace has effected within, preferring to talk about the things of God to God alone. If a man's spirituality has not taught him to restrain his tendency to self-revelation it has not advanced him far. If outward silence is recommended to him in order to prevent him from talking unnecessarily about outward things, an inward silence should be learned which will put a ban upon his talking about his spiritual state when there is no particular need for him to do so.

Lord, teach me to be sparing in my words. Let me learn from your own silence before Pilate and Herod that silence is a quality to be prized. Grant that when I speak I may do so with a certain economy born of prayer, recollectedness, reserve. I cannot imagine a saint who was garrulous or unconsidered in his speech. Let me take my example from the saints and from you.

IF THE CHURCH'S ENEMIES could advance examples of saints who were anxious and fussy, or else could point to sinners whom ✝ SERENITY nothing could perturb, they would be able to do great damage to our faith. Though serenity may not be one of the marks of the true Church, it must surely qualify as one of the marks of true sanctity. This is not to say that it is the surest way to holiness, because charity and humility are the surest way to holiness, but it is to say that it is one of the first things to appear when the way to holiness has been discovered. As a condition for setting out it has its value, but this is nothing to the value it acquires as a consequence of faithful travel. From what may be a natural disposition to begin with, serenity finishes up as a disposition of grace.

Combining in itself such various qualities as hope, confidence, joy, detachment, control of the senses and emotions, few characteristics recommend

131

themselves so readily as this kind of calm to those who are either looking for truth or needing encouragement and comfort. People detect in it all the more reassuring elements. They know that recollection, experience, suffering, understanding and compassion have gone to the making of a harmony which is something quite different from worldly poise and worldly security. People find in the serene man of God the complete man—the balanced individual which in the original conception he was meant to be.

Writing of St. Antony the hermit, St. Athanasius gives the picture which might serve for others besides the subject of the biography: "Being unruffled in soul all his outward expressions of feeling were free also from perturbation, so that the joy of his soul made his face cheerful, and from the gestures of the body might be understood the composure of the soul." Just as the Spirit of God when expressing itself to man is, as Elias was granted to learn, a tranquil movement, so when the same Spirit is allowed its unrestricted way in the soul its manifestation is also tranquil. The soul does not respond to God in the violence of a tempest but in the steady direction of the will. Where every activity is controlled by grace, is at one with the activity of grace, there are no jarring elements left to create disturbance. We cannot imagine our Lord in a state of tension or agitation; we cannot imagine Mary straining to master her worries. There is little enough that we know about Christ's or his mother's manner, but our instinct tells us that their every gesture reflected the serenity of their minds. The mind that is united with the Father's will enjoys a peace which radiates peace. We like coming in contact with holy people because we know that something of their radiance can be caught by us, and that we shall enjoy something of their tranquillity.

Lord, let me not be satisfied with the aloof indifference which often goes for serenity. The kind of serenity which I want by your grace to cultivate is not the majestic quality which can result from studious training in deportment. There is nothing superior about the gift which crowned the spirituality of the saints. Grant that I may so model myself upon the pattern of sanctity, yourself, as to become increasingly of your mind and bearing. I ask for this gift not because my friends will see in it a winning side to me which they had not noticed before, but because I want to be in a better position to resist temptation, help others, and dispose myself for a more single-minded service of your name.

WE ARE SOMETIMES SO EAGER to acquire the fundamental virtues and avoid the fundamental vices that we take too little trouble about what lies on the fringe of both virtue and vice. We know that charity is the fulfilment of the law: very well, we make straight for the essence

✠ TOUCHINESS

133

of charity and set small store by habits of courtesy, congratulation, condolence, which are expressions of charity. We know that pride is the most dangerous of all evils: very well, we attack self-assertion and the spirit of rebellion while forgetting that touchiness, resentment of neglect, the desire for small attentions can be evidence—evidence disregarded—of our mistaken approach.

Over-sensitive natures are obviously more tempted to this evil of taking offence than the thick-skinned, but it is not wholly a matter of natural temperament. If I am expecting to be insulted at every turn it is not necessarily because I am sensitive; it is because I am suspicious. I would not be suspicious if I were more supernatural in my outlook. I may be thick-skinned or I may be thin-skinned, but if I am suspicious of people's motives I shall see hidden meanings in everything that they say or do, and will feel slighted when anyone but myself is praised. The supernatural outlook of faith would cure all this.

The aspect of pride which is immediately responsible for the tendency to complain of affronts to my dignity is my false sense of dignity. Our Lord had more claim to dignity than anyone who has ever existed, was more affronted than anyone who has ever existed, but there is no complaint on his part that this dignity was the side of him that was outraged by man's sin. The moment our pride inclines us to believe that we deserve the esteem of our fellow men we expose ourselves not only to the supposed indifference of other men but often also to their ridicule. We become pompous, petty figures of fun. The man who has most right to the esteem of others will be the last man to demand it. He will also be large-minded enough not to feel the least resentment when it is denied him. It is only the small-minded, the people who are always looking at their little selves in the hope that by noting every inch they may promote their own growth, who notice slights. For such people the slights, whether real or imagined, spell misery.

Lord, I renounce all title to the attention which does not come to me through the channel of charity. When people make a fuss over me out of kindness, I will accept their act of generosity as being directed through myself to you: it is to you that they are ministering and I pray that your love may be pleased and that theirs may be rewarded. But I do not mean to go out of my way to attract this attention, still less to canvass for worldly respect. If I am forgotten, so much the better for me. If I am positively slighted I will try to detach myself from all sense of injury, from the least desire for revenge, from the hope that at least some among my friends may see me as the martyr. If my work is belittled I will try to remember how the work which you did on earth was received. If my motives are questioned, misunderstood, falsified, I must again try to see in all this an opportunity of

identifying myself with your life on earth. Grant
that I may come to prefer neglect and injury to
recognition and praise—and this not in any spirit
of masochism but quite simply because it was the
way which you yourself chose. Grant that, with
you, I may rise above the pettiness of the self-
regarding into the liberty of the saints.

ONE REASON WHY the tendency to scruples is difficult to correct is that so often it is given the credit
for being a trial of the spirit—
✠ SCRUPLES is identified with the dark night
of the soul. Thus entrenched,
scruples refuse to show themselves for what they
are. When a sin becomes respectable it finds a hundred backers who will be so sure of its virtue that
to attack it is taken to be a sign of vice. So respectable can scruples become that souls who are not
troubled by them are apt to wonder if there is anything wrong with their spiritual state; some are
even persuaded, for the sake of conformity to the
orthodox pattern, that they are martyrs to this
purifying affliction when in fact they have never
had a scruple in their lives.

Once the distinction has been made between a
delicate conscience, which shrinks from all appearance of sin that is real, and a scrupulous conscience,
which is one that insists upon eliciting fear of sin
where no sin in fact exists, it should not be too
difficult to train and respond to a delicate conscience while exploding the deceits of one that is

136

scrupulous. In developing a right conscience we need only to recognize three principles: the natural law, the supernatural law, and that application of the natural and supernatural law as seen in the life of Christ. The law, natural and supernatural, tells us how life should be lived; the Gospel shows us how, in the light of the law, it actually is lived. These are the sources of reference in our formation of a right conscience. Without them our conscience will be impulsive and not properly regulated. It is our common mistake in this matter of conscience to think of it as wholly a thing of instinct when in reality it is something which has to be shaped by our knowledge of truth. We talk loosely of "nature" providing us with a conscience, and up to a point this is true. But nature should not be allowed to mould our conscience or it will tend to sanction all natural instincts and belittle all supernatural attractions. It is important to remember that we are ourselves responsible for the formation of our consciences. "My conscience lets me do this." Yes, but has it any right to? If I have a false conscience I have nobody but myself to blame. Now scruples suppose a knowledge of the law together with a false fear of the law. A scrupulous man is not straight with the law; he is straight only with his conscience, which happens to be a crooked conscience. It is no use being conscientious if your conscience is disobedient to known fact. The scrupulous man, then, is not the humble, law-loving, over-obedient soul who he appears to be: he is the obstinate man who trusts his own opinion against authority; he is the man who lacks not only the spirit of obedience but who places fear above love, who places instinct above faith.

Lord, let me not be so foolish as to canonize this weakness. By so doing I must play right into the hands of the devil who will do his best to extend the area of falsification. Grant that I may rely upon the light of your grace which enlightens me through your law, and which enables me to develop the instinct of conscience along the course of truth. Let not any false fear lead me to self-direction, but let me so love your truth that I may be willing to humble myself before the objective expression of it. "Let not the imperfect be afraid," said St. Augustine, "only let them advance." May I advance in your service beyond the reach of this imperfect fear.

THE FALLING OFF in zeal which at times we notice in ourselves can be put down to a number of causes.

✠ TEPIDITY Our confessor will probably tell us that we are unwell, that we need a change, that it is a trial sent by God. The test of such advice must lie in what happens when we are well again, when we have had our change, and when enough time has elapsed to suggest that if it is a trial sent by God the tendency to listlessness is now becoming the kind of habit which calls for direct attention.

Tepidity is more often than not the result of low ideals and low standards. The man who restricts his purpose to doing moderately well will find himself so disappointed with his achievement that his enthusiasm for the work will ebb away. If on the other hand a man decides to aim at the heights— not merely doing well but doing as well as possible for the love of God—he will at least be fired with a sense of high vocation. The fact that he is not realizing all that he purposed will not dismay him: he will know that his ideal lies beyond him, and that only the grace of God has carried him towards it. To the idealist a sense of failure acts as further stimulus. To the mediocre a sense of failure makes only for discouragement. In the lives of the saints the greatest graces have often been due to the sense of failure. Rightly handled, discouragement can be turned to humility, hope, fortitude, perseverance, love; wrongly handled, it leads through a lukewarm service to a stone-cold despair.

In practice, then, what are we to do when we can no longer feel the least interest in our religion, when the whole idea of God's service seems to have gone stale on us? The answer is to be found in continuing the acts of religion as though the impulse to produce the acts were as keenly felt as ever. This is true zeal because it is the life of faith. It is drawing upon supernatural and not upon natural or emotional reserves. When, admitting our inadequacy and want of fervor, we turn to God in prayer, offering to him the work which we do with so much dryness and leaving to him the evaluation of our effort, we are making the best of all sacrifices. We are sacrificing our judgment and our will to his judgment and his will. "We have no strength of our own to meet such an onslaught as this," we can say in the words of Paralipomena, "despairing hearts that know not where else to turn, we look to thee."

My prayer to you, Lord, is accordingly not so much for a return of any superficial zest which may have accompanied the works of religion which I gave to you in what seemed to me times of fervor, but rather for the grace of a true devotion which will endure without complaint the withdrawal of enthusiasm. I resolve to continue my works of service whether I feel fervent or dull, knowing that I am tepid only when I decide to be tepid. I know that genuine slackness is an ever-present possibility, and I pray that I may be guarded against it. Only let not a false conception of slackness bring about a state of true tepidity. If you will teach me more of the meaning of love, I need have no fear of becoming slothful in your service: I am more likely, experiencing an access of charity, to be greedy than lazy. Measure out to me, Lord, the degree of zeal which brings greatest glory to yourself; leave my impressions of the matter out of account.

WITHOUT PRAYER my life will be a succession of chance acts more or less the result of impulse, and **✠ PRAYER** at best in the vague direction of God. With prayer my life will assume a pattern, and my acts will follow a sequence suggested by the light of grace. But though I may be well aware of the necessity of prayer in my life, both from the point of view of giving a praise which is due and from the point of view of my own guidance, I may be without any clear idea as to what its practice involves. The following considerations amount to no more than a re-statement of what I probably know already but what I need to know experimentally.

First there is the question of set prayer—the time that I spend on my knees before God—and then there is the question of an attitude of mind created by set periods of prayer and which amounts to prayerfulness in action. As regards the specific performance of prayer there are certain conditions without which no fruitful results can be expected. Thus I must resolve to avoid deliberate distractions, to keep up the practice when the novelty has worn off, to arrange suitable times and places for it, and if necessary supply myself with prayer material in the way of vocal prayers or subjects to pray about. As regards prayerfulness outside the times set apart for the exercise I must try to make the presence of God the element in which my outward life is lived.

Always assuming that the main work in the soul's education is done by grace, we can compare the process of learning to pray with the process of learning a craft or learning a language. Just as manipulative ability comes only as a result of repeated practice, and just as proficiency in a language can hardly be acquired without intensive study, so prayer demands constant renewal and at least a measure of concentrated application. This is not to say that prayer has to be studied as a science — or else only the leisured and the intellectually-minded would be called upon to pray — but rather to suggest that the habit of prayer is to a large extent conditioned by the seriousness with which the act of prayer is treated. Just as the craftsman applies the principles of his craft outside the workshop, as the artist sees beauty without having to think of the rules and canons which he learned as an art-student, as the man who has learned a new language does not consciously translate from his native tongue but thinks in the terms which he has acquired, so the man of prayer is not preoccupied by the grammar and syntax of prayer but passes easily and smoothly from his regular devotions to his exercise of general recollection. The experimental knowledge which his prayer has given him of supernatural values is carried into the rest of the day. The actual awareness that temporal things are but dust and ashes may, when the prayer is over, evaporate. But actual awareness does not matter. Translating the wisdom learned in prayer to the concrete circumstance which confronts him when the man gets up from his knees is what matters. He instinctively appreciates the supremacy of the spiritual over the material world, and responds accordingly—which is prayerfully.

Lord, teach me how to pray. Show me that the test lies not in my feelings of devotion or in my knowledge of a technique but in my perseverance and my generosity. The test of the artist and the linguist is this: what happens when emotion, suffering, excitement intervene? So, too, with me and prayer: does truth survive the moment of counter attraction?

ENVY IS A SNAKE, creeping on its stomach and hissing at its betters. Whether we are envious of other people, of other opportunities, of other ✠ENVY lives, or even of other periods in our own lives, we become meaner for every deliberate act of envy. Though it may be only in the will, the act of envy cramps the soul and weakens the power of attending to the work in hand. It is also, but indirectly, a subtle negation of faith in the providence of God.

The most obvious form of envy is resentment of another's success. Feeling that we have been cheated out of something to which we have as good a right as the next man, we waste our chances of finding happiness and success in our own particular field by sighing for what we see another enjoying.

143

This, in turn, leads us to take a cynical view of both the person whom we envy and of the good which we know we cannot possess. Our fallen nature inclines us to decry the things in which we have failed, and from this to decry the motives of those who have succeeded. "Since we cannot attain to greatness," says Montaigne, "let us revenge ourselves by railing at it." And, less brutally, Aeschylus: "Not all have the nobility of character to rejoice, without a touch of envy, in friend's success."

Envy and jealousy are not the same thing — jealousy being a matter involving the affections rather than the position or possessions of another— but they can produce the same effect: the mind is driven back upon itself and tries to find a bitter satisfaction in its sense of injury. Jealousy, because it is more personal than envy, is more painful than envy. The sufferer torments himself, and knows while he does so that no good can come from it. "All the tyrants of Sicily," wrote Horace, "never invented a worse torture than jealousy."

But the most idle and short-sighted of all envies are those that have for their object the life unattainable—when we pine for what would mean a different existence altogether. For a married man to envy the life of the monk, for a monk to envy the freedom of the cowboy, for the tubercular patient to envy the activity of the missioner: for these there is need to study the implications of faith. Is God so indifferent to our capabilities and happi-

144

ness that he places us in a way of life which precludes the expressions to which we feel ourselves so powerfully attracted? Does he not plan our environment according to our potentiality? Would it not be contrary to his own interests, let alone contrary to ours, if his infinite wisdom were to arrange circumstances which would only frustrate us when all the time there existed another set of circumstances which could bring out the best in us and make us happy?

We must live by faith and not by fancy. It is sheer fancy to imagine that with the upbringing, the income, the talents, the platform and the public which we so much envy in the case of others we could do better either for God or for ourselves. Nor should we look back into our own past and see there a happiness to be envied. Certainly we can, and should, try to renew the state of mind which was ours when we served God more generously than we do now. But it is a waste of time to wish ourselves back in that earlier setting.

Lord, let envy have no place in me. Grant that I may learn to congratulate others in their success, and be content in my own case with what you have given to me. If I do this I shall be enjoying true success, and will have no cause to envy anyone.

SINCERITY IS SOMETHING more than forthrightness. We have come to think of the sincere man as the genuine, honest-to-God un-

✠ SINCERITY complicated Christian who speaks his mind. But this idea of the no-nonsense extrovert is not the idea of the ancients. The derivation of the word gives as good a definition as any of sincerity. *Sine cera*—without the wax which was used by Roman sculptors to disguise the flaws in a piece of marble. The sincere character is not the one which has no imperfections; it is the one which does not try to cover up its imperfections with counterfeit perfections. Sincerity is not by itself either greatness or holiness, but greatness and holiness could hardly exist unless there were sincerity as well. "The grandeur of the soul does not consist in flying high," says Montaigne, "but in walking orderly; its grandeur does not exercise in grandeur but in mediocrity." The writer is not making a bid here for mediocrity; he is making a bid for "walking orderly"—or as St. Paul would put it "walking sincerely before God." So long as we are sincere before God and man, we are no worse off for living lives that are externally commonplace: our "grandeur," like the beauty of the bride in the *Canticle*, lies within.

The enemy of sincerity is accordingly the parade of sham excellence. If sincerity is truth to the type designed by God, insincerity is that kind of lie which twists God's conception of our nature into the shape which we have conceived for ourselves and which tries to persuade other people to see us so. Our insincerity builds up a false personality, and then seeks occasions for confirming the impression in the minds of others. Lacking the stature to live up to the impression given, we have to compensate by boasting of the great things which we would do if we were given a chance. We are not content with day-to-day goodness: we must dazzle with our heroism, our unique insight, our tender charity, our sanctity. There comes a stage when we cannot be sincere about anything, even to ourselves. The hypocrisy which was assumed in order to hide our weaknesses from others has become such a clinging garment that it hides them from ourselves—and has itself become invisible. When our friends point out our insincerity they get little out of us beyond the grudging admission that we may have been inconsistent or indiscreet. We cling to the idea of sincerity, as we cling to the idea of loyalty, long after the idea has been exploded by contrary practice.

Lord, let me walk before you in truth. Show me the flaws in my character, and prevent me from plugging up the gaps with wax. I cannot hide my true self from you who made me, and I do not want to hide either from my fellow men or from myself. Grant that from the absolute conformity which you bore on earth to the Father's will for you, from the perfect pattern of truth which you presented, I may learn to live in your image and likeness. The more I come to find myself representing the model set by you, the more I shall come to realise my true identity. If I could be truly Christ-like I would be perfectly sincere; it is only because I pretend to be Christ-like, while not taking to the steps to show your attitude towards life, that I am a hypocrite. From your flawless perfection, Lord, grant me the grace of this special integrity and simplicity of outlook, expression, and ideal.

SIMPLICITY GOES WITH SINCERITY. But though one may not be had without the other, it would be a mistake to think that they

✠ SIMPLICITY are the same thing. Sincerity is the absence of artifice; simplicity is unity — the undivided purpose, the single eye. Ecclesiasticus shows us what simplicity is where he attacks its opposite: "Woe to them that are of double heart . . . and to the sinner that goeth on the earth two ways . . . a heart that goeth two ways shall not have success." Simplicity in the present context is more than the unreflecting mentality of the immature or unimaginative: it is, in its spiritual sense, a cultivated unification of powers which directs itself towards God.

The grace of true simplicity leads a man to see the essentials of life and to concentrate upon them. The superfluous does not interest him. Instead of worrying about a multitude of purposes he reduces his program to a formula. The questions which he

148

asks himself are: What is my objective? What is in the way of this? What shall I need? The simple man wants only the will of God, and when he is assured that he is in the way of finding the will of God he makes no fuss about the rest. He works to the best of his ability, and is not discouraged when he finds that his work turns out to be a failure. He is not content with his achievement but he is not discouraged by it. He may know himself to be a failure, but his simplicity secures him against disappointment. He knows that only if he allows himself to be disappointed can he be a disappointment: he can be an outward failure without having allowed any concessions whatever to self. It is concession to self that the simple man has set his heart against: he has not set his heart against failure because success and failure are not in his control. So in the name of simplicity why should he worry?

Proof against disillusion, cynicism, defeatism, the man who has learned to be simple has found the answer to almost all the hideous complexes which modern psychology sees to be tearing at the foundations of mental peace. If I can place my peace in Christ, and live upon the truth that the state of grace supposes this peace, I am supported by both grace and conviction where otherwise I would be dependent upon my own powers of calming down the emotions. If I know that the kingdom of heaven is within me, my outlook is simple. I seek first the kingdom of God, and all these things are added to me. If my will is simple, I shall remain unaffected by complicated outward conditions. I may have a complicated intellect, I may have complicated problems to face, I may be surrounded by complicated people who look for complication in life, but if my will is simple in its purpose I shall ride through all this as though it were a spider's web. In an over-sophisticated civilization and in an over-analytical age the gift of true simplicity is much to be prized and prayed for.

Lord, deliver me from the mental and spiritual hair-splitting which endangers the directness of my vision. I can become obsessed by the work of sifting motives, multiplying resolutions, projecting possible situations and arming myself against a hundred dangers. Grant that I may see life, natural life as well as the supernatural life, in unity. Let me have greater faith, so that I may come to that attitude of simplicity which surrenders all to you. Once I have really handed myself over to your unhampered action in my soul, I shall know a unity within which no external division can disturb. Lord, that I may be one as you are one.

IF DISILLUSION ABOUT OURSELVES is prevented by allowing no illusions about ourselves, dissatisfaction about the will of God is

✠ SUBMISSION avoided by allowing no satisfactions about his service which he does not himself provide. Only when we have completely surrendered to the will of God, surrendering our own ideas about what his will ought to be, are we secure against disappointment. If we fail to submit ourselves in this way we shall go on experimenting in happiness—in a happiness which is not meant for us—and always in the end coming up against the wall of God's will. We can get tired of knocking our head against a wall, and the time comes when we cease to look for happiness or anything else. We just sit about and care no longer. We wait for something—anything—to happen, but we no longer feel the energy to make it happen. Thus it is that the wrong sort of submission can take the place of the right sort, and where surrender to God's will brings both happiness and holiness, surrender to fate brings inertia and sometimes even despair.

The solution to the problem of living can be found only in making the right submissions of the will: submission to the order imposed by the wisdom of God; submission to human authority as representing the divine will; submission to our own limitations. The quest for a solution is made easier in the degree to which we are prepared to surrender our own privately conceived plans as to how we are to achieve our destined place in God's scheme in favor of the plan outlined by God for us. God gives us his plan for the fulfillment of our purpose and so often we think we know a better one. Shall the vessel dictate to the potter, telling him that he is getting the shape wrong? If we go on long enough raising our voice in protest and gratuitous advice, we cease to hear the spinning of the wheel and we assume that the potter has lost interest.

Letting ourselves be moulded by the wisdom of God is the only way to true sanctity—let alone to true happiness. It assumes all the necessary virtues, particularly faith and humility. In its actual practice from day to day, the virtue most needed for the sustained exercise of surrender is patience. Patience of a high order is required to go on waiting for the fruits of our effort when all that can be seen is barren waste. We need patience in relation to God's action which is seldom hurried and hardly ever recognized, patience in relation to human authority which is seldom felt to be sympathetic and hardly ever well enough informed, patience in relation to ourselves because we know that we cannot be relied upon. "Patience," says St. Augustine, "is the companion of wisdom." It is not itself wisdom, but it walks with wisdom and obeys wisdom's command. Since wisdom's command is always to submit the will to the limitations imposed by Providence, patience must needs keep up.

Lord, only show me your will and it is enough for me. I surrender. And in this surrender let me not be content with taking the line of least resistance, submitting for the sake of a peaceful life, but rather let my surrender be the spur to renewed activity in your service. In abandoning myself to your will, I see all the more reason, not less, for trying to make the most of its manifestations. Lord, let there be no quietism in my surrender, but rather let there be the ordered activity of grace.

WE HAVE SEEN THAT, not only for the attainment of perfection but also for the attainment of peace, the human will must bow in ready acceptance of the divine. From St. John's Gospel we learn the lesson in the subjection of Christ's human will to his Father's. "I come to do the will of him that sent me," repeated almost like a refrain, is endorsed by the claim to the possession of a true peace such as the world cannot offer. The submission to the Father's will is given its counterpoint, moreover, in the words from the cross: "I have finished the work which thou gavest me to do" and "It is consummated." But we must notice the medium of expression: subjection to the Father *through* the pressure of created authority. The human will bows not only to the divine will as the divine will but to the human will as standing for the divine will.

It is a mistake to think of obedience as restricted in its obligation to the religious and the family life. It is an essential principle of the Christian life, and touches us at every point. Though its overall demand is, as already noted, related to God, its immediate demand may come to me through the State, through one of the services, through an employer, through the officials of a university, school, society. These are so many channels of grace, and it is for me to use them as channels for the return journey of my response. The higher in the scale of being the authority which commands, the more absolute in the scale of responsibility the obedience which I must give. This does not prevent my obedience from being equally meritorious—it may even be more so if it calls for an exercise of greater faith —when it is given to an authority lower down in the hierarchy of human wills.

So much for obedience to authority when it is a straightforward issue of command and response. But what if the issue is complicated by a conflict between conscience and lawfully constituted authority? The non-Catholic might answer here that in such a case conscience, as representing the voice of God, must be followed. The Catholic would say that since conscience can be formed on the wrong lines, the voice of God cannot always be said to speak through it. The Church is ready enough to champion the cause of conscience against the abuse of authority, but she is not ready to champion conscience against the use of authority as such. Conscience must be very sure that what is commanded is morally wrong, is against the law of God, before the right is claimed to disobey.

Conscience and authority are not only designed to work in harness but unless one or other makes extortionate demands are found in fact to agree.

History and personal experience alike will show that where authority has become corrupt, conscience has somewhere or other failed to protect its rights; and where authority has justified itself, the rights of conscience have been respected. Nothing illustrates this more clearly than the treatment of conscientious objectors during war. The question of harmonizing the respective claims is helped when we recognize the distinction between the respective functions of conscience and authority. Authority is mainly concerned with laying down principles, conscience with applying them. By accepting the principles and acting upon them we answer the requirements of both law and inner light. Faith enlightens the principle, obedience satisfies conscience. "Conscience may stick at the explanation," says Father Bede Jarrett, "but it has to leave the principles alone." Lord, give me a right-ordered conscience and the spirit of obedience to all authority that is recognized by you.

GRATITUDE TO GOD for his gifts is more than spiritual good manners. It is a sign of grace, and, when

✠ GRATITUDE

it becomes the habitual disposition of the soul, a sign of perfection. Certainly where gratitude is not, the other virtues are possessed by the sheer mercy of God and imperfectly.

Gratitude is like the reflector in a lighthouse: given the light, it spreads the light and magnifies it. Without the light it would be nothing—a material thing of no value. The recognition of God as the author of all excellence, and as the donor to the soul of particular excellences, raises the natural instinct to a supernatural level. Its act becomes the act of prayer, and prayer expresses itself in the element of constant, if assumed, thanksgiving.

True gratitude does not stop short at telling God that his gift has been most welcome; it proclaims gratitude in a way which brings others to see and acknowledge. Solomon bore witness to a special gift from God when he wrote for the benefit of others that "wisdom is better than all the most precious things, and whatsoever may be desired cannot be compared to it."

If in dealing with one another it is our human experience that gratitude invites a repetition of the gift, it is our spiritual experience that in dealing with God we invite by our grateful attitude further manifestations of his generosity. This is St. Bernard's doctrine where in a sermon on the Canticles he says: "For it [gratitude] opens the fountains of piety, and moves God to pour himself out upon us. Ingratitude on the other hand dries up the fountain of piety, the dew of mercy and the streams of grace."

Gratitude makes us not only want to share our gift with others but also want to protest our unworthiness of the gift: we want it understood that the gift is not our own but that it has been lent by God, and that we have nothing to be proud of

156

in enjoying its use. We are not possessors, still less inventors, and we hold the gift in a loose grasp in case God may see fit to take it away again. Humility is the necessary consequence of gratitude, and it is the kind of humility which is not likely to lead to discouragement. The humiliation occasioned by rebukes, misunderstandings, disappointments and failures is always likely to suffer from an element of despondency. The humiliation occasioned by the gifts of God lead only to confidence and further gratitude.

Lord, you have loaded me with every kind of grace, and I come before you to say how little I deserve them but how grateful I am. Please do not allow my faulty dispositions to stand in the way of further grace, and may I share with others the good which I have received. I know it to be a scholastic axiom that "every excellence which a man hath is given to him for the benefit of his fellow men." Let me then use the gift according to the mind of the giver—myself becoming, like you, a giver.

Let me take my place with the one leper who gave thanks from among the ten who were cured. I have been healed, sheltered, forgiven, equipped with more than enough to make me holy and happy. I stand before you now with the request that one further grace may be added to the rest: may I know how to use your gifts to your greater glory and the sanctification of my soul. Lord, I give thanks for your great goodness.

Sᴛ. Pᴀᴜʟ ɢɪᴠᴇs ᴜs ᴏᴜʀ ᴛᴇxᴛ for this when he tells the Corinthians that he "most gladly will spend and be spent" for their souls.

✠ GENEROSITY   True generosity is not self-regarding but is out-going and indifferent to the thought of reward. False generosity looks to the opinion of others rather than to their need. It is no good being generous if the one who benefits most is yourself. The applause which is looked forward to by the giver is often of more value to him than the gift which he gives. If you want to be generous towards God or towards people you must try to forget about applause. The right hand must forget what the left hand is giving or it will pick up a trumpet and announce the act.

It is not easy to be generous without being self-conscious. Not easy to have a pure intention in giving. Perhaps the best way is to look at the principle of divine generosity and so to let the thought of self-interest be shamed away from personal generosity. Human liberality is only lent to us from God; it is only a dim and distant echo of perfect liberality as found in the imparting of God himself. Each Person in the Blessed Trinity shows a particular giving, and from each soul a particular giving is elicited. God gives himself, gives all. It is accordingly for us to give ourselves, to give all. As the Father gives to mankind the Son, and as the Son leaves with mankind his Spirit, and as the Spirit gives us grace, so we have the chance of replying with a threefold recognition which is summed up in the total gift of self. In filial service we adore the Father, in attempting to follow his Gospel we adore the Son, in responding to the life of grace we adore the Holy Spirit. The fullness with which we give ourselves to this work of adoration will be the measure not only of our generosity but of our sanctity. Our fidelity comes as a grace from God, our generosity comes as a grace from God, our sanctity comes as a grace from God. Our wisdom lies in referring all this to where it belongs, our folly in appropriating it to ourselves.

When we read that Christ loved his own "unto the end" we must understand the words as meaning not only unto the last moment of his life but unto the limit of generosity. Greater love than his no man had. He emptied himself, becoming obedient even to death. Nor was this act of absolute giving a gesture for our edification merely; it was done for our sakes because we need to make a return in the same kind of giving. "In this we have known the charity of God because he has laid down his life for us; and we ought to lay down our lives for the brethren." This is our practical pattern; here is our test. How does my so-called generosity measure up to the self-giving of Christ? "Thou oughtest not to be so sparing, even of what is thine" is St. John Chrysostom's reproach, "but when thy Lord's goods are committed to thee, why art thou so close-fisted?" *All* that is mine belongs to God; I possess *nothing* that has not been committed o me. I am close-fisted because I am a hoarder, because I have not enough charity, because I am still so weak in faith that I do not draw upon the infinite supplies which the life of grace opens up to me.

Lord, give me a new understanding of generosity. Let me not confine my idea of it to sending expensive presents to people whom I like. Show me that real generosity is something deeper, wider, more Christ-like. Show me that living for others as you, Lord, lived for others is true generosity. I give now not I, but Christ giveth through me.

CHRISTIAN COMPASSION IS THREEFOLD: compassion towards Christ in his Passion, compassion towards others in that their

✠ COMPASSION sufferings are seen as reflections of Christ's sufferings, and compassion for those who are suffering in purgatory. Compassion is co-suffering. It means more than pity. It is the virtue which is not satisfied with distant appreciation but must climb out of the state of non-suffering and get down among the suffering which it sees, and try to share it for the comfort of the one who is afflicted.

Apply this to the sacred Passion and you see that compassion expresses itself in two ways: through the medium of prayer and through the medium of the members of Christ's mystical body. Where compassion is withheld by his disciples, Christ treads the winepress alone. "I looked for one who would grieve together with me," says the Psalmist in prophecy, "and there was none; for one that would comfort me and I found none." Since Christ has, in the words of Isaias, "borne our infirmities and carried our sorrows," it is for us to volunteer in our prayer to be fellow sufferers with him in his supreme act of expiation and compassion. "If we suffer with him," says St. Paul to Timothy, "we shall also reign with him"; there is no guarantee that we shall reign if we have refused to suffer.

Next there is the sympathy which in a practical and effective way we must show to our suffering fellow men. If we deny active compassion to those whom we see, how shall we possess any real compassion for Christ whom we do not see? We may not distinguish between Christ and his members, between the head of the body and the cells of the body. When a limb suffers, it is the body that suffers—it is Christ suffering. This is no academic theory; it is the basis of charity's realistic approach. The Christian is asked to look at his fellow Christian squarely in the face and to see there the challenge of Christ who said that so long as we performed our corporal and spiritual works of mercy towards men we were in fact ministering to him. The more obvious need may be that of the suf-

161

ferer's body, but there is also the need of the soul to which we must minister. We must show compassion by sympathy, suggestion (if asked for it), example, and prayer.

Lord, impress upon my mind that the absence of compassion in my religious expression is quite enough to disqualify me from all possibility of holiness. I may hate sin, have a love of prayer, be ready to embrace flamboyant penances, and give careful attention to my work. But together with all this there must go a tenderness for sinners, sufferers in mind and body. Show me that if I pretend to be trying to model myself upon your pattern, compassion for the unfortunate must be an essential in my life. In my inferior measure and degree I want to reproduce your readiness to share the sufferings of others and to share the merit of your own suffering with other people.

And at this point I can consider the third of the three aspects or objects of compassion. I can ask God to let the fruit of my sufferings be joined with the fruit of his in bringing comfort to the souls in purgatory. My desire is not to hoard whatever merit I may gain by patient endurance, but to spend it in the same spirit that Christ gave out to all mankind the infinitely perfect fruits of his endurance. Lord, do with my sufferings what you will. Only let not the imperfect dispositions in which I suffer be an obstacle to whatever use you have in mind. Let me be a channel of compassion to others.

SOME THINGS ARE GOOD because they are commanded, others are commanded because they are

✠ LOYALTY
good. The reverse is also true:
some things are wrong because
they are forbidden, others for-
bidden because they are wrong. Even if the Church
made no bid for our loyalty, we would know that
loyalty was due. Loyalty, like mother-love, is a
recognized good. The scholastic view that nature
does not act on impulse or without purpose gives
direction to an instinct which might otherwise re-
strict itself to partisan feeling. Devotion to the particular community to which we belong has its roots
in the conception of man and its fulfillment in the
service of God.

Ideals can be devalued, standards lowered, instincts turned to perverse expression, but when a
cynical generation has done its worst on loyalty
there is an agreed nobility in the act of remaining
faithful to, and proud of, an institution, a person,
or a cause. The strongest argument in favor of loyalty is the fact that everyone wants it. But argument is not everything; we need incentive as well.
A man may know all the reasons why he should be
faithful to his wife, but unless he accepts the principle of fidelity he may well stray into infidelity.
Whether to a wife or a country, to the Church or
to Christ himself, loyalty must be allowed its right-
ful place in the complete man, in the complete
Christian. For Christians the incentive is there,

163

where we would expect it to be, in Christ. Loyalty has been sanctified by Christ. Christ wept over Jerusalem because he was part of it and it was part of him. He was loyal even to the Jewish priesthood, which he attacked for being disloyal to his Father. He was loyal to the Jewish people, which was divided precisely in its loyalty.

Our loyalty to the Church, to the country to which we belong, to one another, is to be given in union with Christ's loyalty as practiced on earth. Only when we have seen this point of view can we begin to talk about Christian loyalty; only when we have seen this point of view can we judge what loyalty is not. Loyalty does not mean unthinking subservience but calculated self-giving. The loyal patriot or religious or husband does not have to blind himself to the flaws that exist in the object of his loyalty; he has to remain constant, *flaws and all.* It is easy enough to be loyal when my government acts as I think it should, when my superior or partner chooses what I would choose and asks of me what I feel inclined to give. The test of loyalty is not in agreement but in disagreement, not in approval but disapproval. If, making allowances for mistakes, failures, prejudices, I am staunch in my allegiance I am gaining in strength and charity. If I decide to look beyond all this area of difference for an affinity discoverable perhaps by faith alone, I am practicing loyalty. If I enter into a holy complicity with the good which I know must

164

be there while detaching myself from the temporary and accidental evil which I see, I am loyal. It will mean, too, that I am learning to appreciate the parable of the wheat and the cockle.

Lord, let my loyalty reflect your own. That is the first thing I ask. I ask also that it may go deeper than the external expression of fidelity. Grant that I may have the generosity to remain constant not only when the public gaze is turned towards me but when you alone are witness to my thoughts. Let me in mind be loyal, and the effort to be loyal also in speech and action will follow.

ALL RELIGIOUS PEOPLE would agree that our security must rest in God. "Cast all your care on God, for he hath care of you" ✠ SECURITY and "the Lord ruleth me, and I shall want for nothing." Trust is one of the first conditions of the religious response, deepening as the spirit of religion develops in the soul until the climax is reached in perfect love. But we must get this idea of trust right; we must not confuse it either with recklessness, which is the sign of presumption, or with superstition, which is the sign of false fear. Perhaps the best way of investigating security in God is by investigating insecurity among creatures.

Insecurity can be a weakness or a strength, according to whether it drives us to find support in material things or in divine grace. The evil side of insecurity is more evident than the good side because human nature tends more to fear than to confidence. The human imagination makes us more vividly afraid when insecurity threatens than it makes us look forward to ultimate rest in God. Psychologists attribute to insecurity almost all the compulsions to which human beings are liable: drink-compulsion is seen as escape from the uncertainties of life, food-compulsion as the desire to eat everything within reach now in case there will be nothing within reach later, the hoarding compulsion, the compulsion that drives one person to take more and more sleeping tablets in case he should not "secure" his regular hours of sleep and another to get up long before the dawn so that his prayers and devotions may be "secure" against the calls upon his time later on in the day—all these manifestations point to a fundamental lack of balance and support. People who are more or less confident in going on as they are will be less prone to accumulate against a rainy day; they will also be less anxious to escape into unreality. If insecurity makes for compulsion, security makes for control. We must be secure upon the foundations supplied by our faith; only thus can we be properly balanced and at peace.

The fruits of this supernatural security are almost too obvious, and are certainly too numerous, to mention. Detachment from luxury and worldly pleasure, independence of the emotions, readiness to accept afflictions, refusal to admit defeat in prayer, recognition of the spiritual significance in human affairs, calmness and recollection. "If I should walk in the midst of the shadow of death," the soul can say with the Psalmist, "I shall fear no evil." All fortitude rests on the security of hope. "Neither wisdom nor justice is of any worth without the security of fortitude," wrote St. Bruno, "and what shall I say of it? How shall they be called strong who cannot hide the heart's emotion?" The same saint says also, "Fortitude is never conquered, or if conquered is never fortitude." True security, in the same way, is never lost; or if lost is never true security.

Lord, I place my whole security in you. Only when your love and your will are the grounds of my confidence am I proof against disappointment and disillusion. It is because I am not disinterested enough, not secure enough in what you have promised me, that I lose my head in panic and doubt. Considering how unreliable I have proved myself to be, it is strange that I still look to my own ingenuity to provide those insubstantial things in which men place their trust. I renounce this exercise as lacking in supernatural faith. In you I trust, and am no longer insecure.

"WHERE COURAGE IS NOT," Dr. Johnson is reported as saying, "no other virtue can survive except by accident." The important word here is "survive," not "accident." The implication is that moral courage is needed if the virtues are not to die off from the fear of exercising them as virtues. It is a doctrine of which St. Paul would have approved. For the practice of Christian virtue there has to be a degree of indifference to worldly opinion amounting to supernatural fortitude, and sometimes even to heroic sanctity. "If the world hates you," says our Lord himself, "know that it hated me before it hated you." Without the courage of our convictions we shall come to doubt our convictions; given this courage we shall retain not only the convictions themselves but the means both of developing them within ourselves and of imparting them to others.

+ MORAL COURAGE

Courage can be stirred by fear, music, liquor, the desire for notoriety or to shine in the opinion of one whom we wish to impress, and by the sheer determination to be tough, but unless it looks to God for its motor force it wastes itself on mere staying power when it might be endurance for Christ. Where ordinary courage may act on impulse, moral courage acts on the combined influence of faith, conviction, and grace. Where all forms of courage are sustained by hope of some sort, Christian courage is sustained by a particular kind of hope which is a mixture of faith and love. Indeed Christian courage is an expression of the three theological virtues to which its existence bears witness.

In the face of socal and intellectual opposition, the man of moral courage pursues the course of truth as he sees it. He may be misunderstood as to his motives, he may be ridiculed, he may shrink from having to take the line he does, he may appreciate the loneliness of the struggle which lies ahead of him, but he has measured all this against the weight of truth and has made his decision. Scorn for his critics is not going to help him to persevere. Even the sense of doing something worth while will not be enough to keep him at it indefinitely. The only influence strong enough is confidence in God. Back again at hope. Hope and moral courage are so closely connected that the only difference seems to be that where hope looks at the ultimate triumph, courage looks at the immediate need to triumph. Hope looks chiefly at God and only perforce at creatures, courage looks directly at creatures in the knowledge that all help must come from God.

Give me the courage, Lord, which will refuse to compromise with the world. Religious principle and practice are entities fixed by you and I must not allow the world to exercise its pressure. I am not ashamed of the truth which I hold from you; I will not hide it nor water it down. By pretending that I do not know the Catholic view, by saying that I think the Catholic standard demands too much, by hiding my own Catholic identity or by condoning the action when I see others hiding theirs, I show myself to be a moral coward. As one baptized and confirmed I carry with me all the graces needed for the public confession of my faith. Lord, let me draw upon these graces and face the world without hesitation or shame. I know that if I am ready to confess your name before men, I shall receive the reward of having my name confessed by the Father in heaven.

EVERYONE HAS HIS OWN IDEA about holiness and what a saint should be like. Perhaps we attach too much importance to what we think of sanctity and not enough to what God thinks of it. If we

✠ SANCTITY

want to know God's view we know where to look. The Incarnation is the "en-fleshment" of the final word of sanctity. Consequently for us sanctity can be nothing else than the re-presentation of the Incarnation in the setting of our own particular lives and within the range of our own particular temperaments. When we find Christ we find sanctity; when we re-live his life we partake of his holiness, share his thought, enjoy his merits, communicate his doctrine and his love. For the Christian there is only one sanctity because there is only one Christ. A hundred different saints do not produce a hundred different sanctities according to their hundred different natures; they reproduce the one sanctity of him who is the model. "There is no other name under heaven by which man may be saved—*tu solus sanctus.*" Each saint responds in his own way, but the response he gives is that of charity. God is charity, and the saint is the one who perfectly gives to God that which is God's—that which is God himself. All saints agree on one quality, and that one quality is the qualifying mark of their sanctity: it is charity, it is Christ. They may differ from one another in their asceticism, in their prayer, in their humility and poverty. But while God never said that he was asceticism, prayer, humility or poverty, he did say that he was charity. *Deus caritas est.* And he did say that he was Christ.

Applying all this to my ordinary life with its ordinary round of pleasures, duties, devotions, temptations and apparently waste spaces, I must ask myself whether the life of charity is really the target of my endeavor, whether I have seriously proposed to myself the Christ-life. Does charity rule my decisions? Is Christ's patience reproducing itself in me? Am I tolerant, truthful, just, gentle *because these qualities are in the mind of Christ?* Or do I show these qualities only when it suits me to do so, and as coming from myself rather than from him? Do I value sanctity because of its appeal or because it represents Christ? Do I look more to what people may think of my sanctity than to what

God may think of it? Do I look upon all human virtue as merely borrowed from him or do I think myself responsible for its achievement? Do I allow myself the satisfaction of watching myself grow in virtue, bettering others in the competition? Do I regard myself as conferring a favor upon God in trying to become holy—as it were paying him a compliment by responding to his summons? If I am honest in answering these questions I shall be in a better position to assess the nature of sanctity in general—the true sanctity which is Christ's—and of the sanctity to which my own self-esteem lays claim.

Lord, the source and end of all holiness, teach me the meaning of sanctity. Let me have no other thought about it but what is yours. Let me strive after it only for the greater glory of your name. If I could be holy for my own sake and not for yours I would be holy in vain. Not for its own sake or mine, but for you alone do I want to be holy. Grant me to persevere in pursuit of holiness, and show me how it is not to be found in works, devotions, and practices, but simply in the love of you.

Part 2

Occasional
Prayers

Acknowledgment

The works from which prayers in this section have been quoted are the *Missal,* the *Breviary,* the *Rituale,* the *Raccolta,* and the *Holy Trinity Book of Prayers.* The lives and writings of the saints have also, as in the first part of the book, contributed many passages to the text. It has not been thought necessary, in a devotional work of this sort, to give the references. Where neither name nor source appears under a paragraph, the prayer is the author's.

O Lord Jesus Christ, who has said, "Ask and ye shall receive, seek and ye shall find, knock and it shall be opened unto you,"

✠ FOR DIVINE LOVE grant we beseech thee unto us who ask the gift of thy most divine love that we may ever love thee with our whole hearts, words, and works, and never cease from thy praise.

Prayer from the Litany of the Holy Name

Let our mouths be filled with thy praise, O Lord, that we may sing of thy glory because thou deigned to make us partakers of thy holy, divine, immortal, and life-giving mysteries; preserve us by thy holiness all our days that we may learn thy righteousness. Alleluia. Alleluia. Alleluia.

St. John Chrysostom

Let us beseech the Lord that the participation in his holy rites may be for us the turning away from every wicked thing, for our support on the journey to life everlasting, for the communion and gift of the Holy Spirit. Amen.

Liturgy of St. James

Assist me, my Jesus, for I desire, whatsoever it may cost, to become good. Take away, destroy, utterly root out all that thou findest in me contrary to thy holy will. At the same time I pray thee, O Jesus, to enlighten me that I may be able to walk in thy holy light.

Blessed Gemma Galgani

O GOD, before whom every heart lies open and to whom every desire speaks and from whom no secret lies hidden, cleanse the thoughts of our hearts by the pouring forth of thy Holy Spirit so that we may merit perfectly to love thee and worthily to praise thee.

✠ FOR A PURE INTENTION

The Missal

MAY THE POWER of thy Holy Spirit, O Lord, be present we beseech thee unto us, cleansing our hearts in thy mercy and defending them from all harm.

The Missal

PURIFY WE BESEECH THEE, O Lord, our consciences with thy visitation, so that when our Lord Jesus Christ, thy Son, shall come to us he may find a dwelling prepared for him.

The Missal

ALMIGHTY GOD, take from me all vainglorious thoughts, all desires for mine own praise, all envy, covetousness, gluttony, sloth and lechery, all wrathful affections, all desire of revenge, all delight in harm to others, all pleasure in provoking them to wrath and anger, all delight in upbraiding them and insulting them in their affliction and calamity. Give freely unto me, good Lord, thy love and favor which my love for thee, be it ever so great, could not receive except out of thine own great goodness.

St. Thomas More

IN FAITH AND PURITY let us stand before the altar of God. Not with scruple or offence, not with guile or fraud, not with wiles or deceit, not with doubt and not with little faith, but with a right conversation, a pure mind, a single heart, and a perfect faith.

Armenian Liturgy

THERE MUST BE MANY OCCASIONS, Lord, when the works which might glorify your name are wasted by either the vainglory, carelessness, self-interest or superficiality with which I perform them. I pray that my intention may be so purified that every effort of mine may find its true direction and so bring praise to you. Grant that what is wanting to my desire may be made good by the perfection of Mary's intention as she went about her life of prayer and work on earth.

ACCEPT, LORD, THE PRAYERS which I am to say this day and unite them with those of the whole Church. Receive the labors which I am to perform and the sufferings which I am to endure. I know that I shall not possess the presence of mind when the occasions arise, so I make the intention now, in advance, of wanting to please you in every action, every decision, every enjoyment and every disappointment.

IN UNION WITH YOUR OWN WORK for souls as you preached in Palestine, let me go about my work among men. In union with your own prayer to the Father during your life and Passion, let me pray.

HEAR, O LORD, MY PETITION and suffer not my soul to faint beneath thy chastisement. Let me not

✠ FOR PERSEVERANCE slacken in confessing to thee the loving kindness whereby thou didst rescue me from all my evil ways. Be thou sweeter to me than all the allurements which I once pursued, so that I may love thee with all my strength . . . so that I may be delivered from all temptations even unto the end.

St. Augustine

O LORD OUR GOD, in the covering of thy wings do we hope, and do thou protect us and bear us up. Thou bearest us up when we are little ones, and even to our old age shalt thou bear us up. For when thou art our strength, our strength is strength indeed; but when it is our own it is but weakness. With thee liveth always our good, and when we are turned away from thee, we are turned to evil.

St. Augustine

GIVE EAR UNTO OUR SUPPLICATIONS we beseech thee, O Lord, and direct the paths of thy servants in the way of thy salvation, so that amid all the changes of the journey and of this our life, we may be protected by thine aid.

The Breviary

EVERYWHERE WE ARE IN CONFLICT; everywhere there are temptations and snares. Deliver us, we beseech thee, from our enemies; defend us from

178

all dangers to the soul and to the body, Lord, that at length we may come to thy eternal rest.

St. Bernard

How HIGH THOU ART in the height, how deep in the depth. Thou never leavest us, yet how hard it is to return to thee. Come,

✠ **FOR ZEAL** Lord, and work. Arouse and incite us. Kindle us and sweep us onward. Be fragrant as flowers, sweet as honey. Teach us to love and to run.

St. Augustine

O MY SWEET SAVIOUR, Christ, while thine undeserved love to man would suffer the painful death of the cross let me not be cold or lukewarm in my return of love to thee. And grant, most blessed Redeemer, that I may strive after those things only for which I ought to pray unto thee, and to keep from me all those things for which I ought not to pray. And to thee, and to the Father, and to the Holy Spirit, be all honor and glory world without end. Amen.

St. Thomas More

LORD, STIR THE HEAVINESS of my mind and heart so that I may serve you with a better grace. I know myself to be by nature indolent and quickly cooling in enthusiasm; let me by an increase of your grace show zest in what I undertake, imparting to others the fire that your love must light in my soul. SPARE ME, LORD, from the sin of serving you with listless hands. Give me so acute an awareness of my opportunity that even in the works which outwardly seem to be of no account I may find material for supernatural dedication.

THOU, LORD, ALONE HAST POWER over life and death. Thou hast shown wonders of old, and hast

✝ FOR
SALVATION

delivered thy servants out of great peril. Thou didst save Isaac lying on the altar, and Joseph from the hands of his brethren. Save me, too, for thy name's sake. Amen.

St. Theodulus

LET THE ABSOLVING WORDS be said over me, and the holy oil sign and seal me, and thy own body be my food and thy blood my sprinkling. And let my mother Mary breathe on me, and my angel whisper peace to me, and my saints smile on me . . . that in them all and through them all I may receive the gift of perseverance, and die, as I desire to live, in thy faith, in thy Church, in thy service, and in thy love.

Cardinal Newman

HAVE MERCY, O GOD, and save me from everlasting death. Have mercy, O God, and for all my sins and crimes grant me true penance and pardon. Have mercy, O God, and grant me remission of all my sins so that thou mayest rescue me from all tribulation, free me from all uncleanness of heart and body, extinguish in me every spark of lust, and deliver me from all the wiles of the devil and from all evil. . . . Almighty God, do thou vouchsafe to bless me with an everlasting blessing, for thou, O God, art blessed, ineffable, unchanging for ever and ever. Amen.

Alcuin

✠ **FOR THE CONVERSION OF SINNERS AND INFIDELS**
THAT THOU WOULDST VOUCHSAFE to bring back into the unity of the Chruch all that stray, and to lead all unbelievers to the light of the Gospel, we beseech thee to hear us, O Lord.

Litany of the Saints

O GOD, WHO BY WASHING AWAY the crimes of the guilty world in water didst shadow forth the figure of regeneration in the very outpour of the deluge that the mystery of one and the same element might spell both the end of vice and the source of virtue, look down on the face of thy Church, O Lord, and increase and multiply thy regenerated people.

The Sarum Missal

ETERNAL GOD, CREATOR OF ALL THINGS, be mindful of the souls of infidels, created by thee and made after thine own image and likeness. Behold, O Lord, how to thine dishonor hell is filled with these same souls. Remember that for their salvation Jesus, thy Son, did suffer a most cruel death. Permit no longer, I beseech thee, that thy Son be despised by infidels, O Lord, but being appeased by the prayers of holy men and of the Church, be mindful of thine own mercy and make them one day to know him whom thou hast sent, the Lord

181

Jesus Christ who is our salvation, life, and resurrection.

St. Francis Xavier

SINCE IT IS YOUR WILL, Lord, that the sinner should not die in his sin but should be converted and live, I pray that to the soul of every sinner may come such an abundant grace that conversion can no longer be delayed.

LORD, I PRAY for this soul's conversion. May the truth of Catholicism become so evident that all doubt be dispelled. Let the discovery and conviction be followed by such an earnest desire to come into the Church that all practical obstacles may be swept aside. Finally I pray that the reception into the Church may be sealed and crowned by the experience of true peace in Christ.

✠ FOR A PARTICULAR CONVERSION

LORD, HERE IS ONE who needs the help of your grace. Give light and strength, I beseech you, and do not allow this soul to listen to the excuses which may be advanced by the devil for rejecting your persuasion. Sinners do not know what is best for them; souls in the darkness of unbelief cannot imagine what it is like to enjoy the true light of faith; those who are floundering in the bitter waters of obstinacy are at heart craving for the peace which you alone can give. Lord, whatever at present stands in the way, convert this soul to the life of grace.

FOR THE CONVERSION of this soul, Lord, I trust more in your grace than in any argument, example, or prayer of mine. When I have done all I can towards helping another in the discovery of peace and truth there is still the comforting knowledge that, when my effort has come to nothing, your grace is the only effective factor in the story of every conversion. Lord, bring your grace to bear upon this soul, and may the conversion which is brought about give satisfaction to your Sacred Heart.

MAY ALL WHO DENY Christianity in this land come to see the error of their argument. May all who

✚ FOR THE CONVERSION OF OUR COUNTRY

profess Christianity come to live in accordance with the doctrines of the Gospel. May all who look elsewhere than in Christ for the solution of their soul's problem be led by the Holy Spirit to the only possible answer.

LORD, WIN OVER THE MINDS of our countrymen so that all may acknowledge you as the way and the truth and the life. Having seen and believed in your divinity, may they see your spirit, truth, and life in the one true Church which you have founded.

MAY THE EVILS of false ideologies gain no hold upon the minds of men in this land. Grant that all the members of this much-blessed nation may belong to the one Faith, confess to the one Lord, and generously act upon the one Gospel. Lord, convert our country.

LORD, I SEE that a civilization can be Christian in name while keeping far from you in heart. I see your seamless coat being torn into many pieces. I see within the Christian allegiance such discords as must sadden your Sacred Heart. I see divisions in belief as well as in charity; I see jealousies, apostasies, and standards which are of this world and not of the Gospel. Let neither sectarianism, paganism, agnosticism, atheism, nor sheer indifference hinder the spread of truth in this country. Lord, bring about a heartfelt conversion among these souls whom you have redeemed.

IN PRAYING FOR THE NEEDS of the Church, Lord, I ask particularly that those who are in a position

✝ FOR A CHRISTIAN LITERATURE

to influence others by the written word may be filled by a sense of mission in their work. Grant that journalists, novelists, playwrights, historians, and also those writers whose field is more strictly religious, may be guided more by the Holy Spirit than by considerations of publicity, fashion, and material reward. Grant that all who write may think more of their vocation than of their career.

LORD, I PRAY that the press throughout the world may take on a more principled character. I pray that in Christian countries the publications that pour from the printers may not be ashamed to declare the Christian tradition and uphold it. Instead of sensation and scandal let there be justice, truth, and purity. O Holy Spirit, give to publicists, politicians, broadcasters — to all who have a hand in shaping public opinion—a sense of their responsibility before God. Contemporary writing will not be slow to reflect the change.

SINCE IT IS MOSTLY by what they read that men are educated, I pray that those who write may supply material for the formation and development of truly Christian thought. Lord God, Wisdom itself, grant to the writers of our generation and country the wisdom to put down on paper only what is in accordance with your holy will. Let not their selfishness spoil the work which may so well be wrought by you through them.

LORD, I PLEAD before you the cause of Christian art. Give to those who have either the creative ability or the taste which others are prepared to accept, the light to put their talent to an apostolic use.

✠ FOR A CHRISTIAN ART

Let them come to see so deeply into true beauty as to want only to impart that vision to others for the glory of God and the appreciation of truth. Help them, Lord, to draw the public's attention to the source of beauty, to the source of truth.

I PRAY NOT ONLY that the purely secular artists

and craftsmen may come to a more spiritual conception of their responsibility but also that those who work in the name of religion may resist the tendency to destructive criticism, jealousy, acceptance of low standards, complacency, and to thinking solely in terms of financial gain.

IN THIS MATTER of religious art, Lord, I pray for two classes of people: those who claim to know nothing about it, and those who feel confident to pronounce. May the former be given the humility to learn the principles from the latter, and may the latter be given the humility to explain these principles without arrogance. May the standard of art be thus raised from the tawdry to the true, and so bring praise to you who are truth itself and beauty.

MAY THE CREATIVE ARTISTS of our time, we beseech you, O Lord, come to realize that they enjoy the privilege of reflecting your own creative activity. Let their minds be so filled with this idea of their vocation that the works of their hands will bear the marks of your inspiration.

IF OBJECTS OF CREATED BEAUTY have the power to raise the human mind to you in praise, may such works be multiplied by the artistic activity of man. I pray also that, the prejudices of many being removed, men's minds may respond to the authentic good which is revealed by those who are given the opportunity of unveiling it.

186

LORD, SINCE MORE THAN at any other period in history the stage is judged to be an effective medium of contemporary thought, I pray for the integrity of dramatic art. Grant that from the theater, the screen, the ballet, and the opera may come the note of Christian truth. Banish, Lord, the evils from which these art-forms are suffering: false ideology, suggestiveness and amorality, the music and movement of the jungle. Let the breath of your Holy Spirit blow fresh air through every department of the drama.

✝ **FOR A CHRISTIAN DRAMA**

IF DRAMATIC ART can be divided according to whether the appeal is to the head, to the heart, or to the body, then I pray that you may provide equally against intellectual error, erotic sentiment, animal passion. Substitute for these influences the principles of faith and morality which, through the means of the theater, will go far to raise the standard of human conduct. Whether serious or frivolous, the world of entertainment needs to be founded on principles and not on the lack of them.

GRANT TO PERFORMERS, script-writers, and producers a feeling for something more than the ability to cause surprise. Give them the desire to convey what is best to their public, not merely what is most arresting. Reveal to them the chances that are theirs, show them the significance of their talent, let them see the implication which attaches to

187

their work. Lord, stir the players by your Spirit so that the playgoers may in turn be stirred.

HAVE MERCY, O LORD, on all those whom thou hast associated with us in the bonds of friendship and kinship, and grant that they, together with us, may be so perfectly conformed to thy holy will that being cleansed from all sin we may be found worthy, by the inspiration of thy love, to be partakers together of the blessedness of thy heavenly kingdom. Through our Lord Jesus Christ thy Son who with thee liveth and reigneth in the unity of the Holy Spirit, God world without end. Amen.

✠ FOR FAMILY
AND FRIENDS

Gallican Sacramentary

DEFEND, I BESEECH THEE, O Lord, through the intercession of the Blessed Mary ever Virgin, all those who are joined to me in blood, kinship, acquaintance or affection, and all my benefactors and enemies, from every danger of body and soul, open or hidden, and grant to them the grace which they most need, whatsoever it be, that being made firm in thy love, they may never be separated from thee by temptations but may attain to everlasting life. Through Christ our Lord. Amen.

The Missal

ALMIGHTY AND MOST GRACIOUS GOD, have mercy on *N* and *N;* have particular regard and consideration for all my friends, and for each and every one of them as godly affection or occasion may require.

St. Thomas More

I PRAY, LORD, FOR THOSE who belong to me by ties of blood and to whom I belong in friendship, duty, or debt of gratitude. Remind me constantly that next after my loyalty to you, my concern lies with those to whom you have immediately related me. Only when I have given to my family what is due can I start thinking about my obligations towards others. I pray for the members of my family, Lord, and beg you to grant each of them the grace of final perseverance.

LET YOUR OWN HOLY FAMILY be my inspiration in the handling of my family responsibilities. May I see in the household at Nazareth the solution to the domestic problems which face me at every turn. Grant to us from your own home the graces of mutual understanding, mutual confidence, mutual assistance. In body and soul may the members of my family be free from harm, and may they make it their first business to give praise to you.

LORD, LET THE LOVE which I bear to the members of my family be a sincere love: let it not be exploited by me for my own convenience but let it be for your greater glory and for the good of the individual souls. My relatives have not been selected, moreover, at random: they have been chosen out from among countless millions as being suited to one another and to me for our common purpose in your plan. Let us realize this destiny together, they and I, putting no obstacles in the way of your grace.

LORD, BLESS THE HOUSEHOLD of which I form a part. Show us how we can help one another, share our interests and sorrows and joys with one another, be ready to make sacrifices for one another. I ask that I may find my joy in serving them as you found your joy in serving Mary and Joseph on earth.

LORD, I PRAY for someone who is dear to me and who is sick. May the sufferings which this soul is to endure be to your glory and to the salvation of the soul concerned. Let the trials of illness be accounted for penance, and, whatever the issue, let your will be accepted in the best dispositions of humble and loving resignation.

✝ FOR ONE WHO IS SICK

LORD, IF MY PRAYER can contribute to the recovery which I so earnestly petition, may no condition be wanting to my attitude in making the request. Accept my offering, my hope, my willingness to suffer. Lord, hear my prayer for this person who is sick.

MARY, REFUGE OF SINNERS and help of the sick, be at hand in this illness which is causing so much anxiety and pain. May you watch over this soul, praying that God's will be perfectly realized in whatever turn the disease may take. I pray for complete recovery, but if God has other plans, I beseech you, most holy Mother, to dispose both the sick person's soul and mine for whatever it is that he wants to come of it.

St. Camillus, patron of the sick and dying, grant to this friend of mine who is struggling for life the generosity to yield health, life, comfort, hopes for the future, and every earthly care, entirely to the Providence of God. Pray for me too, that I also may be resigned to whatever results from this present crisis.

✠ FOR WORLD PEACE — Eucharistic Heart of Jesus, furnace of divine charity, give peace to the world.

The Raccolta

Give peace in our times, Lord, for there is none other that fighteth for us but only thou, O Lord our God.

The Missal

Graciously give peace in our days, O Lord, that being assisted by the help of thy mercy, we may ever be free from sin and safe from all disturbance. Through Christ our Lord. Amen.

The Missal

If men would only obey your laws, Lord, there would be no wars to disturb mankind. If nations only trusted one another in times of peace the threat of further outbreaks would be removed. Lord, bring home to the minds of men — to the leaders and the led alike — the need for charity, confidence, and obedience to your will.

Lord of peace, give a true and lasting peace to the world. Grant that all nations may come to see that peace is not to be found in the balance of

191

power and the force of threat, but in submission to the gospel of peace—in submission to you. Where one nation sees peace in terms of temporal security and another in terms of empire, let Christian countries see peace as the gift of God. Lord, let the world enjoy true peace—having earned it by the acceptance of your Gospel.

O GOD, WHO WILLEST that all men should be saved and come to the knowledge of the truth, send we

✠ FOR VOCATIONS

beseech thee laborers into thy harvest, and give them to speak thy word with all confidence that thy message may run and be made plain, and that all peoples may know thee, the only true God, and him whom thou has sent, Jesus Christ thy Son our Lord, who with thee liveth and reigneth in the unity of the Holy Spirit, God, world without end. Amen.

The Missal

LORD, RAISE UP BY THY GRACE a generation of saintly priests and religious who will present your Gospel to the world as it is meant to be presented. May those who are engaged in the apostolate be men of mortified life and single purpose; may they be so faithful to your word which it is their vocation to preach that men may be attracted to the truth. May those who are called to the hidden life respond so generously to the spirit of their order as to bring down upon the Church your grace and pardon.

WE PRAY THAT SOULS may feel drawn to leave the world in order to pray and suffer for the world in the obscurity of the religious life. May the appeal of the hidden apostolate attract many whose generosity might otherwise attach itself to unworthy objects. Grant that those who are hesitating in their choice may see the beauty of prayer, self-sacrifice, and the vows of religion.

ALMIGHTY AND EVERLASTING GOD, have mercy upon thy servant *N.,* our supreme pontiff, and direct him according to thy loving kindness in the way of eternal salvation, that of thy gift he may ever desire what is pleasing to thee and may accomplish it with all his power.

✠ FOR THE POPE

The Missal

O GOD, the Shepherd and Ruler of all thy faithful people, mercifully look upon thy servant, *N.,* whom thou hast chosen as the chief shepherd to preside over thy Church; grant him, we beseech thee, so to edify both by word and example those over whom he hath charge that he may attain to everlasting life, together with the flock entrusted to him.

The Missal

LORD, JESUS, shelter our holy Father the Pope under the protection of thy Sacred Heart. Be thou his light, his strength, and his consolation.

The Raccolta

GRANT TO THE PRESENT POPE, Lord, the virtues which he needs for his tremendous office. Let him have the humility to resist the voice of flattery, the patience to endure the tedium of interviews, the charity to give his endless audiences, and the zeal for spiritual things which will keep him always close to you in the midst of his many distractions.

ALMIGHTY AND EVERLASTING GOD, who workest great miracles unaided, send forth upon thy servants and upon the flocks entrusted to their care the breath of thy life-giving grace, and let thy blessing never cease to fall like dew upon them so that they may please thee in truth.

✠ FOR GOOD LEADERS

The Missal

ALMIGHTY GOD, we pray that thy servant who by thy mercy has undertaken the government of this country may receive increase of all virtues, the fit adornment of a ruler, enabling him to withstand every foul temptation and to be welcomed at the last by thee who art the way, the truth, and the life.

The Missal

LORD AND RULER of the universe, appoint to positions of leadership, we beseech you, men who will listen to your word. May they take their principles from you and not from the standards of the world. Let them not make their decisions according to opportunism, greed, personal ambition. May

194

they govern the peoples under them in charity, justice, and dependence upon your Holy Spirit.

IF IT IS TRUE that countries are given the governments which they deserve, grant that we, the subjects, may merit to have good leaders over us. By our professed dependence upon your strength, by our example in private and public life, by our prayer and charity, let us develop so Christian an environment within the State that those who are called upon to govern may reflect, and in their turn promote, the Christian ethic.

✝ FOR A
PARTICULAR
INTENTION

O GOD, our refuge and our strength, who art the author of mercy, hearken to the pious prayers of thy Church, and grant that what we ask in faith we may faithfully obtain.

The Missal

GRANT, WE BESEECH THEE, almighty God, that the intercession of holy Mary, mother of God, of all the holy apostles, martyrs, confessors, virgins, and of all the elect, may cause us everywhere to rejoice; that while we celebrate their merits we may experience their patronage.

The Missal

LORD, YOU HAVE TOLD US that we were to ask, seek, and knock. You have told us also that what we prayed for in your name would be granted us by the Father. You have told us further that our petitions would be heard according to the meas-

195

ure of our faith. Lord, I address my request to you today in the terms suggested by you when on earth you instructed your disciples in prayer.

AWARE THAT MUCH is wanting to my disposition, I come to you in confidence and hope and love. I believe that supplying what I lack, you will look not at what I deserve but at what you are prepared to grant. In your name I ask for this favor, and if it is to the glory of your name I know that you will bless my request.

THERE IS URGENCY in my petition, Lord, and though there is almost certainly an element of selfishness in my imperative desire, I nevertheless pray with all the faith, hope, and love which I can call up from a heart which is sadly deficient in these dispositions. I offer you the best I can do, and pray that you may reward the offering from the limitless store of your love.

LORD, I AM MOVED by a strong desire which I refer in the spirit of earnest hope to you. I know that you alone can grant me the answer to my request. If the desire is according to your will, may it be purified and rewarded. If it is not according to your will, may it cease to weigh with me and may a more worthy desire take its place. You know what it is that I want, but what you want is more important than my ardent wish. Not my will, Lord, but yours be done.

MY PETITION is laid before you, and I come to await your decision. In the light so far received

I see only my side of the question at issue and to me it seems a matter of great importance. I can well believe, however, that there are other sides which I do not see and that these may have greater claim upon your generosity. If my request is to be denied, Lord, grant me the grace of accepting humbly your decision and waiting upon the next manifestation of your will.

LORD, I CANNOT DO WITHOUT your help in this emergency. Come to me with the solution which I so earnestly request. If other needs are more vital, or if another solution is more to your honor than the one which I am praying for, I pray that you may exercise your divine wisdom regardless of my entreaties. My concern is to pray as I see it right to pray, yours to give grace as you see fit to give it. Your will be done.

ALMIGHTY AND EVERLASTING GOD, in thy goodness release from the bondage of sin thy servants who

✠ FOR GRACE
TO OVERCOME
A FAILING

plead guilty in thy sight. Let the pain of remorse which is their punishment be outweighed by thy gracious mercy which brings them pardon.

The Missal

O GOD, who, far from wishing the sinner to perish, grantest the wicked the grace of pardon, we humbly beseech thy gracious majesty to guard and keep with heavenly aid and constant protection thy servants relying upon thy mercy, so that they may serve thee always and not be severed from thee by any trials.

The Missal

O GOD, who turnest all things to the advantage of those who love thee, implant in our hearts such an undying love of thee that no temptation may have power to alter the desires which are born of thine inspiration.

The Missal

EXPERIENCE HAS SHOWN ME where my greatest weakness lies, and I come to you for the strength which is needed to correct it. In fear I recognize the danger to my salvation which this weakness signifies. I know that unless I attack it with greater resolve I shall be at the mercy of an abiding evil. Lord, be my strength. Lord, quicken my resolve. Lord, take command of me once for all and put an end to this habit of mine which temporizes with what I know to be inconsistent with your will.

MY PREVAILING TEMPTATION is humbly laid before you, Lord, and I ask for greater courage in dealing with it. In penitence for past failure, and in full trust that your grace will work to better effect in the future, I stand before you and implore your help. I am under no delusions about myself. Unpromising material that I am, I offer you all. Bring about, I pray you, so real a transformation in my will that I may no longer make concessions to my lower nature.

LORD, I SURRENDER to your law and repudiate

all selfish rebellion. So train me in self-discipline that my practice may draw into line with my principle. I know that such a change in me will not, short of a miracle, be effected overnight. I know that I must co-operate with every prompting of grace. I know that I must keep watch, must be ready to do battle, must refuse to be either discouraged by failure or lulled into complacency by success. Lord, help me before the failing becomes part of my nature.

CONSIDER MY WEAKNESS, O Lord. See the catalogue of my failures, O Lord, and bring me new life and hope. As I value my sanctification I ask for the grace to overcome this obstacle to the development of your love in my soul.

LORD, WHOSE WORD brought instant calm to the waters which threatened the safety of Peter's boat, say but the word and my soul will be calmed. As in the case of the disciples, so in my own case: the quality which is lacking is that of faith. Looking less at my own ability to handle the situation I must trust more in the power of grace. It is because I am of little faith that I am in constant danger of being submerged. Lord, save me or I perish. I know that you watch over our safety and that there is nothing to fear when you are with us. Lord, I have confidence that you will speak to the waves and bring about in me a great calm. Then let me make use of the tranquillity to give you praise, undivided service, thanksgiving.

GRANT UNTO US, Lord Jesus, ever to follow the example of thy holy family that in the hour of our

✠ FOR A HAPPY DEATH death thy glorious virgin Mother together with the blessed Joseph may come to meet us and we may be worthily received by thee into everlasting dwellings. Who livest and reignest world without end. Amen.

The Missal

O DEARLY BELOVED Lord Jesus, by all thy labors and sorrows, by thy precious blood and sacred wounds, by thy last words on the cross . . . we most earnestly beseech thee to deliver us from a sudden death. Grant us, we pray, room for repentance. Grant us a happy passing in thy grace, so that we may be able to love thee, praise thee and bless thee for ever. Amen.

The Raccolta

BEING UNCERTAIN WHETHER I shall have command of my senses when I depart from this world, I offer thee now my last agony and all the sorrows of my passing. Since thou art my Father and my Savior, I give back my soul into thy hands. Grant that the last beat of my heart may be an act of pure love toward thee.

The Raccolta

O GOOD JESUS, I offer thee the last day, the last hour, the last moment of my life. May I die loving thee with thy holy love. May my being and my life be sacrificed and consumed for thy glory, and may my last breath be an act of pure love of thee.

St. John Eudes

O GOD WHOSE MERCIES are without number, to whom only it belongeth to heal after death; who art the life of the living, the hope of the dying, and the salvation of all that trust in thee, do thou cleanse the soul of thy servant, *N,* from all sins by virtue of thy sacrament and deliver it from all pains.

✠ **FOR ONE RECENTLY DEAD**

The Sarum Missal

I PRAY FOR THE SOUL of one who was dear to me on earth and whose salvation means much to me. May this soul be soon relieved of the pains of purgatory so that the joys which you have prepared may, by our efforts here on earth, be hastened.

COMFORT, WE PRAY YOU, Lord, the soul who has come before you for judgment. Grant that the punishment which is due may be speedily undergone, and that the light of your glory may not be withheld an instant longer than is necessary. May this soul remember me in the day of release and in the eternity of joy which follows.

LORD OF LOVE, let not your love for the sinful and suffering be restricted by our unworthiness. This soul for whom I pray may not be worthy of graces for which I ask; I myself am certainly unworthy of having my requests granted. But it is not a question of what we deserve: it is a question of what we need, and pray for, and hope to receive. Lord, grant this soul rest. Grant me also pardon of my own sins so that I may stand a better chance of coming swiftly, together with this soul for whom I pray, to give you everlasting praise in heaven.

O God, the Creator and Redeemer of all the faithful, grant to the souls of thy servants departed the remission of all their sins, that through pious supplications they may obtain the pardon which they have always desired.

✠ FOR THE FAITHFUL DEPARTED

The Missal

We beseech thee, O Lord, that the prayer of thy supplicants may benefit the souls of thy servants, that thou mayest deliver them from all their sins and make them partakers of thy redemption.

The Missal

Grant a resting place to the souls of the faithful in the arms of our fathers, Abraham, Isaac, and Jacob; feed them in a fertile land and by the waters of comfort, in a paradise of joy and in that place from which the broken heart, sorrow, and sighing has flown. Make them rest in that abode, Lord, in the light of thy saints, and do the same for us also who are sojourners on this earth. Keep us in thy faith, and grant us thy peace unto the end. Amen.

St. Gregory

We pray for those who are detained on their

way to eternal joy. May this present suffering be light to them, and may they remember us when they come into their inheritance.

GRANT TO THESE SOULS whose sins are, in the merciful dispensation of grace, being removed in the pains of purgatory an alleviation of suffering; may your love relieve them and may they come soon to the possession of eternal peace.

O HOLY SPIRIT, soul of my soul, I adore thee. Enlighten, guide, strengthen and console me. Tell me what I ought to do and command me to do it. I promise to be submissive in everything that thou shalt ask of me, and to accept all that thou permittest to happen to me; only show me what is thy will.

✠ **TO THE HOLY SPIRIT**

Source Unknown

ENLIGHTEN OUR MINDS, O God, and purify our desires. Correct our wanderings and pardon our defects, so that by thy guidance we may be preserved from making shipwreck of our faith, be kept in a good conscience, and at length be landed in the safe haven of eternal peace. Through Jesus Christ our Lord. Amen.

St. Anselm

GO BEFORE OUR ACTIONS we beseech thee, O Lord, by thine inspiration, and further them by thy help, that every prayer and work of ours may begin always from thee, and through thee likewise be ended.

The Missal

O God, from whom come all holy desires, right counsels and just works, give unto thy servants that peace which the world cannot give; that our hearts being given over to obey thy commandments, and the fear of enemies being removed, our times by thy protection may be peaceful.

The Missal

O Holy Spirit, Spirit of Truth, come into our hearts. Shed the brightness of thy light upon the nations that they may please thee in unity of faith.

The Raccolta

All for thee, most Sacred Heart of Jesus. Heart of Jesus, let me love thee and make thee loved.

✝ TO THE SACRED HEART

Sacred Heart of Jesus, mayest thou be known, loved, and imitated. Heart of Jesus, I put my trust in thee. Divine Heart of Jesus, convert sinners, save the dying, deliver the holy souls in purgatory. Heart of Jesus, protect our families. Sacred Heart of Jesus, strengthened in thine agony by an angel, strengthen us in our agony. Heart of Jesus, I love thee; convert all poor blashemers. Most Sacred Heart of Jesus, have mercy on us.

The Raccolta

Almighty and everlasting God, look upon the Heart of thy beloved Son and upon the acts of praise and satisfaction which he renders thee in the name of sinners; and do thou in thy great goodness grant pardon to them who seek thy mercy in the name of thy son, Jesus Christ, who liveth and reigneth with thee, world without end. Amen.

The Rituale

O HEART OF LOVE, I put all my trust in thee. For I fear all things from my own weakness, but I hope for all things from thy goodness.

St. Margaret Mary

I GIVE AND CONSECRATE myself to the Sacred Heart of our Lord Jesus Christ, my being and my life, my actions, pains and sufferings, so that I may be unwilling to employ any part of myself save to love, honor, and glorify the Sacred Heart.

St. Margaret Mary

HOLY MARY, bring help to the miserable, strengthen those who are afraid, comfort those who mourn, pray for the world at large, plead the cause of the clergy, intercede for devout women. May all who pay homage to your holy name experience your powerful help.

✠ TO OUR LADY

The Breviary

WE FLY TO THY PATRONAGE, O holy Mother of God; despise not our petitions in our necessities, but deliver us always from all dangers, O glorious and blessed Virgin.

The Breviary

GRANT THAT I MAY PRAISE THEE, O sacred Virgin; give me strength against thine enemies and against the enemy of the whole human race. Give me strength humbly to pray to thee. Give me the

205

strength to praise thee in prayer with all my powers
. . . O holy mother of God, flowering as the lily,
pray to thy dear Son for me, a wretched sinner.

St. Anselm

O MARY, VIRGIN MOST POWERFUL and mother of
mercy, queen of heaven and refuge of sinners, we
consecrate ourselves to thine immaculate heart. We
consecrate to thee our very being and our whole
life: all that we have, all that we love, all that we
are. To thee we give our bodies, our hearts, and our
souls. To thee do we give our homes, our families,
and our country. We desire that all that is in us and
around us may belong to thee, and may share in the
benefits of thy motherly blessing.

The Raccolta

O MOST HOLY MOTHER of Jesus, thou who didst
witness and didst feel the utter desolation of thy
divine Son, help me in my hour of need. O mother,
I come to bury my anguish in thy heart; and in thy
heart to seek courage and strength. O mother, offer
me to Jesus.

St. Bernadette

HOLY MARY, our Lady of Deliverance, pray for us
and for the holy souls in purgatory. O heart most
pure of the Blessed Virgin Mary, obtain for me
from Jesus a pure and humble heart. Mary most
sorrowful, mother of Christians, pray for us.

The Raccolta

MARY, I PRAY THAT your place in my life of
prayer and service to God may be what you want

it to be. Let my devotion to you remain constant, sincere, and fruitful in practice. I know from experience that on these three points I am likely to fail. I am inclined to neglect you when not in conscious and immediate need of your intercession; I am inclined to express my response to you in terms which are not always perfectly genuine; and I fail to model my conduct upon the ideal which you represent and teach. Mary, by your own life of prayer and service, help me to direct my life in the straight course to God.

MARY, BE MY ADVOCATE before the throne of God. Grant me to draw from your store of merit so that the poverty of my claim to blessedness may be overlooked. You are the refuge of sinners, the protectress of the poor. Take me under your care and I shall no longer have cause to be afraid.

REMEMBER, O MOST PURE SPOUSE of the Virgin Mary, St. Joseph, my beloved patron, that never ✠ **TO** hath it been heard that anyone **ST. JOSEPH** invoked thy patronage and sought thine aid without being comforted. Inspired by this confidence I come to thee and fervently commend myself to thee. Despise not my petition, dear foster-father of our Redeemer, but accept it graciously. Amen.

The Raccolta

BE MINDFUL OF US, O blessed Joseph, and intercede with thy foster Son for us by the pleading of thy prayer. Do thou in like manner render the blessed Virgin Mary thy spouse gracious unto us, for she is the mother of Him who with the Father and the Holy Ghost liveth and reigneth world without end. Amen.

St. Bernardine

St. Joseph, model of quiet confidence and humble life, pray for me in my moods of anxiety and worldly ambition. Let me trust as you trusted in the primacy of the supernatural over the natural. Let me see in commonplace work the highest implication and opportunity. Let me serve our Lord and his mother as you served them.

Teach me, St. Joseph, the meaning of hard work. From your workshop at Nazareth let me learn the lesson of constant unassuming labor. When I feel tempted to get through my work in an anyhow sort of way, to make excuses for careless performance, to hide the defects of my work from others and show only the good points, send me a sharp message of rebuke. Be with me in every work of mine, St. Joseph, to direct it with a pure intention and unremitting application before the throne of God.

St. Joseph, patron of those who toil at occupations which escape attention, grant that I may work at whatever is given me to do without either dramatizing my effort, trying to attract applause, or indulging in a sense of wasted energy. Let me neither seek to impress others with my industry nor wallow in the bitterness of merit unrecognized. Like you, I want to let the opinions of men take their chance.

O HEAVENLY PATRON, in whose name I glory, beseech God constantly on my behalf. Confirm me in faith; strengthen me in virtue; defend me in the conflict; so that as a victor over the malignant foe I may merit to attain to everlasting glory. Amen.

✝ TO OUR PATRON SAINT

The Raccolta

O THOU, MY MOST SPECIAL patron, intercede in my behalf unto our Lord, that, living according to thy perfect rule and example, I may with thee contemplate the beauty of his face.

Blosius

SINCE I HAVE PLACED MYSELF under your particular protection, I come to you now in respect, gratitude, and petition. Let not my veneration of your name stop short at distant recognition; let not my gratitude be a mere empty form; let not my requests be wholly selfish. Help me to follow your example in loving God, to express my thanks by acting as you would want me to act, to back my frequent petitions with acts of sacrifice and the exercise of virtue. You have not been given to me as an object of superstition but as an object of veneration and imitation: let me be worthy of your patronage and protection.

WHETHER I COME UNDER your care because I happen to bear your name or because I happen to admire the life you led on earth, I know that the relationship is not a chance affair but one which is allowed for and blessed by the providence of God. In his wisdom the Father has appointed to me certain helps towards my sanctification, and you are one of them. I pray that you may prompt me frequently, intercede for me constantly, and let me benefit by your example, suffering, virtue, and prayer.

I PRAY TO YOU, my patron saint, that you would guide me towards the recognition of God's will, the performance of God's will, and the final possession of God's will in the way that you yourself enjoy his will eternally in heaven. Amen.

✠ IN THANKSGIVING

FOR ALL THOSE THINGS which thou h a s t g i v e n to us, O Christ, thou requirest nothing of us but that we be saved. And giving us this very thing, thou thankest the receivers.

St. John Chrysostom

MY GOD, I give thee thanks for what thou givest, and for what thou takest away. Thy will be done.

The Raccolta

ENABLE ME, O my God, to return thee thanks as I ought for all thine inestimable blessings and favors. Thou hast thought of me and loved me from all eternity; thou hast formed me out of nothing; thou hast delivered up thy beloved Son to the ignominious death of the cross for my redemption; thou hast

210

made me a member of thy holy Church; thou hast preserved me from falling into the abyss of eternal misery when my sins had provoked thee to punish me; and thou hast graciously continued to spare me even though I have not ceased to offend thee. What return can I make for thine innumerable blessings, O my God, and particularly for the favors of this day? O all ye saints and angels, unite with me in praising the God of mercies who is so bountiful to so unworthy a creature.

The Holy Trinity Book of Prayers

WHATEVER PRAYERS I USE that have been devised by men, I still cannot thank you with the gratitude that is due. I draw therefore from the infinite merits of the Mass, and offer you thanks in your own words and from your all-adequate sacrifice.

IF THE WORLD MUST still endure, at least gather thou a larger and larger harvest, an ampler proportion of souls out of it into thy

✠   **IN**   garner, that these latter times
ADORATION   may, in sanctity and glory and triumphs of thy grace, exceed the former . . . that we may know thy way upon earth, thy salvation upon all the nations. Let the people praise thee, O Lord. Let the nations be glad and leap for joy; because thou dost judge the people in equity and dost direct the nations on the earth.

Cardinal Newman

211

GREAT ART THOU, O Lord, and greatly to be praised; great is thy power, and of thy wisdom there is no end. And man would fain praise thee, being a part of thy creation . . . thou dost arouse us to find delight in praising thee because thou hast made us for thyself.

St. Augustine

I LOVE THEE, O Jesus, with my whole heart, because thou art infinitely perfect and infinitely worthy of love. Give me the grace never more to offend thee in any way, and grant that after being refreshed by thy eucharistic presence here upon earth I may merit to attain to the enjoyment with Mary of thy blessed and eternal presence in heaven.

The Raccolta

MERCIFULLY HEAR THE PRAYERS of thy people, we beseech thee, O Lord, that we ✠ **IN TIME OF DISTRESS** who are justly afflicted for our sins may be mercifully delivered from the same for the glory of thy holy name. Amen.

The Breviary

HOLY MARY, comfort the miserable, help the faint-hearted, relieve the sorrowful, and pray for thy people . . . may all who venerate thy name feel now thy help and protection. Be thou ever ready to assist us when we pray, and bring back to us the answers to our prayers. Make it thy continual care to pray for the people of God.

St. Augustine

Lord, afflictions have multiplied lately and I come to you for strength with which to endure them. My heart is heavy and I feel hopelessly ill-equipped to meet the demand. From your Passion grant me the grace to stand firm; from your cross grant me the grace to accept. Let me bear no grudge against the people—and still less against the decrees of Providence—which force this situation upon me. Into your hands I commend my spirit.

My present trial must be to your glory, Lord, or it will lose its point. May I see in it the will of the Father, and may I reproduce in its acceptance the mind of the Son. To you, O Holy Spirit, I look for light and love and the necessary generosity with which to suffer my afflictions in a way that pleases the Blessed Trinity.

I know well that it was not so much the injustice of the Roman governor and the cruelty of the soldiers that scourged thee as my sins. O accursed sins that have caused thee so many pains. With what hardness of heart, when notwithstanding thy manifold sufferings for me, I have continued to offend thee.

✠ IN PENITENCE OF HEART

I have sinned, and my sins are always before thee. Yet my soul belongs to thee, for thou hast created it and redeemed it with thy precious blood. Grant that thy redeeming work be not in vain. Have pity

213

on me. Give me tears of true repentance. Pardon me for I am thy child. Pardon me as thou didst pardon the penitent thief. Look upon me from thy throne and give me thy blessing.

The Raccolta

LOOSE, REMIT, AND FORGIVE my sins against thee, O God. Whether in word or in deed or in thought, willingly or unwillingly, knowingly or unknowingly committed, forgive them all. For thou art good, and lovest mankind.

St. John Chrysostom

FOR THE SAKE of the holy mother of God, accept our supplications, O Lord, and save us. Let us make the holy mother of God and all the saints our intercessors with the Father in heaven, that he may be pleased to have mercy, and in his pity to save his creatures. Almighty Lord and God, save and have mercy.

Armenian Liturgy

✠ IN TIME OF WAR

JESUS, KING AND CENTER of all hearts, by the coming of thy kingdom grant us peace.

The Raccolta

GRANT THAT THESE WARRING NATIONS may tire of their hatreds, Lord, and learn the value of true Christian peace. May they cease to envy one another, fear one another, seek to destroy one another. Lord, prince of peace, intervene we beseech you in this conflict which brings such sadness to mankind.

TEACH US INDIVIDUALLY, Lord, the truth about war. Show us its folly, and give us a longing to remain always at peace. Grant that each member of the race, living at peace within himself, may make his contribution to the peace of the world. Give to all the light to see that by obeying the voice of conscience a private citizen can further the obedience of others and so further the peace of the world. I pray for the peace which the world cannot possess unless it accepts it in your terms.

WHILE WE MUST ACCEPT this war as finding a place in the Father's will, we can nevertheless pray that the Father may will it to cease. Grant that those in authority as well as those engaged in fighting may acknowledge the present evil as a punishment for sin, and so call down upon the world the pardon which is only waiting to be pronounced. O God, to fight is an affront to charity and justice. Grant that these hostilities in which we are now involved may give place to the peace which follows the full acceptance of the Gospel. Your Gospel is the Gospel of peace, and in the name of your Christmas message to mankind grant peace on earth to men of good will.

AMONG THOSE ENGAGED in the fighting, Lord, I pray for the protection of those who are dear to me. In body and soul may they be spared the dangers of this war. I pray also for those who are in no fit state to die—that they may survive the present emergency and put their souls right with you.

FINALLY, LORD, I pray about the after-effects of war. Let not the innocent be hardened by their experience. Let not the ideals which you have formed in the minds of men be brought low. Let not the passions stirred up by war debase the moral standards of the post-war generations. It is tragedy enough that cities should be levelled to the ground, but it is still more tragic that principles should be abandoned and that standards of conduct should be reduced to rubble.

MARY, QUEEN OF PEACE, bring this war to an end. Mary, queen of peace, intercede on behalf of sinful man. Mary, queen of peace, protect us from one another and from ourselves.

HELP US, O LORD our God, since we cannot flee from the body, nor the body flee from us. We must needs carry about the body, because it is bound up with us. We cannot destroy it; we are forced to preserve it. But the world surrounds us and assails us through the five gateways of sense.

✝ IN TIME OF TEMPTATION

St. Bernard

LONG PRAYERS ARE USELESS to me when I am under pressure from the devil, from my lower nature, from the enticement of sinful pleasure. I pray quite simply, but quite desperately, for help.

LORD, SOURCE OF STRENGTH, give me strength

216

against the powers of evil. Lord, who resisted Satan in the desert, resist him now again in his attack upon my soul. Lord, whose Passion is the price paid for the redemption of my soul, let not another sin of mine contribute to your pain on earth.

PATTERN OF EVERY VIRTUE, source of all good, be with me now when all the good that I possess is threatened. Lord, perfection itself, let not the perfection which my soul is aiming at be disqualified by the evil which is trying to draw me away from you.

GRANT ME, O GOD, the presence of mind which will let me see the issue as it really is; grant me the grace to remain firm. Awaken in me the love which is stronger than the desire for present satisfaction. Show me how to place all my trust in you.

LORD, GRANT ME the grace of making a good use of this time of sickness. I may not be able to work, and it is unlikely that I shall

✠ IN TIME OF SICKNESS

feel well enough to give long hours to prayer. Let me be frequently reminded by your grace to practice resignation and recollection. Since my present sickness is designed towards my spiritual health, I must, instead of showing resentment, express my gratitude. Not my will, Lord, but yours be done.

HOWEVER ILL I NOW FEEL, or may later come to feel, I can console myself with the thought that no other work of mine is quite so capable of bearing fruit at this present time as the work of gladly accepting the illness which you send.

IF PAIN IS TO BE my lot in the trial that has come to me, it will be a pain exactly measured to the work of my sanctification. Bring to my mind in the course of my sickness, Lord, that nothing of what I have to bear is hidden from you and that at every point you are present with the help of your grace. I firmly believe and trust that my powers of endurance will be made equal to whatever I am called upon to bear.

LORD, I KNOW from experience that when ill I am liable to exaggerate, to indulge the imagination, to become exacting, unreasonable, introspective and self-commiserating. Grant me not only a lively sense of faith which will enable me to see my afflictions as heaven-sent opportunities of grace but also a lively sense of proportion. I mean to take in my stride, relying always on help from you, the upsets of mind and body which this illness must occasion.

MARY, MOTHER OF GOD, be with me in my illness, in my convalescence, in my sleeplessness, and in my periods of boredom and depression. Should God not want me to recover, be with me also in my agony. Pray for me, O mother of God, now and at the hour of my death. Amen.

LORD, MY HEART is as heavy as lead, and I cannot see beyond this present state of depression. I do not

✠ WHEN DEPRESSED ask, since it may not be your will to grant it, for immediate consolation. I ask for an increase of faith, hope, and love. Given more grace, I can endure my mood of passing gloom. I accept it in a spirit of penitence. Lord, turn my discouragement into true humility.

MAY THIS LOWERING of my spirits be to me, Lord, a reminder of my dependence upon your support. If I cannot even master the sense of dejection I am evidently not to be relied upon for the works of heroic sanctity. Show me how to trust in you from moment to moment, from mood to mood, from resolution to resolution. Thus oriented towards you, I shall be better able to rise above my periods of flagging hope.

IF EVEN THE SAINTS were subject to fits of sadness, Lord, I am not surprised to find myself sometimes almost overcome with heaviness of heart. But I should know that there is all the difference between the sorrows of the saints and the melancholy of the self-indulgent. Let me not give way to the movements of temperament, but grant me the grace of seeing in depression a possible occasion of furthering the devil's purpose.

WHILE UNITING MY WEARINESS of spirit with your own agony in the garden, Lord, I unite my will with yours in surrendering to the will of the

219

Father. I ask that this chalice may pass from me, but I ask still more that the Father's will be done.

LORD, GRANT ME the grace to meet this disposition of mine with greater courage. I need an increase in each of the theological virtues: more faith with which to recognize your will; more hope with which to see beyond my present trial; more love with which to present myself to you in the spirit of self-sacrifice.

FROM THE WRETCHEDNESS in which I find myself I do not ask for a spirit of hilarity. If cheerfulness is what you want me to enjoy I accept it gladly. All that I ask is for the strength to continue in whatever state you wish for me. I ask to be spared the possible evils of sadness, and certainly against self-pity, disillusion, cynicism, and discouragement I will fight with all the energy I can muster. Out of the depths I have cried to you, O Lord; Lord, hear my voice.

IF I WERE in closer relationship with you, Lord, I would not suffer these spasms of loneliness. Grant

✠ WHEN LONELY

that when, as now, I feel the ache of being on my own I may enter more deeply into union with you. Evidently I am insufficient to myself: be to me my whole sufficiency.

SHOW ME HOW to approach my sense of being alone and cut off so that it may not be any longer a condition to be dreaded, but rather be seen as a means to closer dependence upon you. Let my soul learn in solitude the lesson of your presence.

LORD, I SHOULD KNOW by now that the only loneliness to be feared is that of sin. Sin isolates more bitterly than distance. But even apart from the loneliness of being cut off from grace there are depths of loneliness which are hard to endure. Grant that without giving way to despair and self-commiseration I may meet such trials and derive the best from their experience. Let me see this present circumstance as a test of love, an invitation of grace, an incentive to prayer. Lord, join me in my isolation and I shall rejoice to be alone with you alone.

IF THIS PURIFYING and humiliating state of mind is to continue, Lord, give me the wisdom to make good use of it. Let it not upset my judgment, drive me to resentment or reduce me to apathy, but on the contrary may it bring me to a new maturity of soul. Grant that out of this present trial I may emerge more independent of creatures, more ready to find companionship with you.

WHATEVER MY FEELINGS in the matter I can appreciate the truth that the loneliness which you allow is for my soul's good. When you separate us from our friends you provide at the same time compensating helps. On those occasions when you allow us to feel most alone you offer yourself most immediately to be the object of our whole love. Lord, if the outcome of my present trial is a more intimate

221

knowledge of you then I am grateful for this grace despite the pain that accompanies it.

IN THE PROBLEM OF SLEEPLESSNESS I find myself alternating between two extremes: either I cheerfully imagine that if the body needs sleep it can be counted upon to see that sleep will come, or else I fall into an unreasonable panic about being unable to get through my work on account of lack of sleep the night before. At one extreme I become reckless, working late and not giving sleep a chance; at the other extreme I become over-anxious, and so stay awake when I might be asleep. Show me how to strike the balance in this matter, Lord, neither neglecting what experience has shown me to be my necessary measure, nor worrying unduly when I fall below this quota. Lord, I trust in your providence to provide me with the rest that is necessary to me if I am to do your will as perfectly as you want it done.

✠ WHEN UNABLE TO SLEEP

O GOD, who in the process of your created work appointed a time of regular rest for man, grant me the physical relaxation of sleep. I do not ask for mathematical regularity in the hours of sleep which you may see fit to let me have, but I do ask that you should let me have enough of it to prevent my nerves from playing me false. I find that sickness is a more straightforward trial to endure than

222

sleeplessness, and if I am not to be defeated by it I shall need much strength from you.

AFTER CONTINUED LACK of sleep, more than after lack of food or drink, my mind seems liable to entertain misconceptions and even to fall into delusions of one sort or another. While I do not ask necessarily that the trial of insomnia be removed—since it may in your providence be the chosen means of my spiritual advance—I do ask that if it is to continue, my sleeplessness may be accompanied by special helps from you.

GRANT ME in this present difficulty to wait in patience for the relief which I know you will bring me when the need is really urgent. Preserve me from the sense of desperation which not only hinders the natural solution to my problem but which prevents me from seeing its supernatural value and purpose. Keep before my mind, Lord, the fact that there are worse evils in the world than not being able to sleep. Preserve for me my sense of proportion, and inspire in me the desire to turn this commonplace affliction into an activity of true penance.

INSTEAD OF MY ORDINARY ACTS of prayer, which I seem to be unable to make, may the desire to pray be acceptable to you, Lord.

✠WHEN UNABLE TO PRAY I know that what matters most in prayer is the will to give you love and praise; this I possess and hereby hand over to you. If the ability to follow up the intention with suit-

223

able expressions of prayer is lacking, I have at least the assurance that you will make good what is wanting and that you will not lack for the homage that is due.

Since I appear to be without inspiration or feeling, I content myself with echoing set forms of prayer as they occur to my memory. Knowing well that your own prayers which the liturgy expresses are of infinitely more value than any which I, even when devotionally at my best, might compose, I repeat with confidence *Te decet laus, te decet hymnus; tibi gloria Deo Patri et Filio cum Sancto Spiritu in saecula saeculorum. Amen.* If these words mean little to me in my present state of dryness, I pray that their meaning may mount up before you and be received in your own terms.

When both reason and authority tell me that it is not the feeling of your presence but the fact of it which constitutes the work of grace in prayer, I should have no cause to despair during this period of incapacity. I believe, even though my emotions refuse their help in this act of belief, that your presence is with me, Lord, and that all in fact is well. Lord, I cannot pray. I know that you can pray instead of me. If I count wholly upon your prayers I shall thus be better off than if I trusted even slightly in my own.

Mary, mother of God and mother also of those who are trying to draw near to God, pray for me. I want to draw near to God, but feel myself far away from him. When I ask you to pray for me, I mean not only on behalf of me—which is certainly among the favors that I ask — but also *for* me in the sense of in my place. Pray when my prayers fail. Speak to your Son when I am silent; speak to your Son of the things that for one reason or another I am unable to speak about. Ask him for what I need; beg his mercy; give him praise. My dryness will not then leave me destitute but on the contrary richer.

MAY THE ALMIGHTY and merciful Lord direct us on the way of peace and prosperity, and may the

✝ WHEN ON A JOURNEY

angel Raphael accompany us on the journey so that with peace, health, and joy we may come back again to our home.

The Breviary

O GOD, who didst cause the children of Israel to pass with dry feet through the midst of the sea, and by the guidance of a star didst open to the three Wise Men the way that leads to thee, grant us we beseech thee a safe journey and tranquil weather, so that in the company of thy holy angel we may be able to arrive happily not only at our present destination but finally at the haven of our eternal salvation.

The Breviary

O GOD, who didst lead Abraham out of Ur of the Chaldees, and didst preserve thy servant from harm on all the ways of his pilgrimage, deign we beseech thee to watch over us thy servants. Be unto us, O Lord, a help in battle, a comfort on the way, a shade in the heat, a shelter in the rain and cold, a sure transport in our weariness, a refuge in trouble, a staff upon uncertain ground, a harbor in shipwreck; so that with thee as our leader we may arrive happily at our destination and at length return safely to our homes.

The Breviary

LISTEN WE BESEECH thee, Lord, and direct the ways of thy servants in the straight course of salvation, that amid all the variations of the journey and of this our life we may be ever protected by thine aid.

The Breviary

SHOW ME BY THE LIGHT of your Holy Spirit how to see in every journey that I undertake a symbol of the soul's course towards you. Let my present experience of travel teach me lessons which will be useful in the journey of life. Let it teach me patience, self-denial, recollection, charity towards my fellow-travelers who are also on the move towards eternal life.

IF I EMBARK upon my journey in a supernatural spirit, I can make of it a pilgrimage and a prayer instead of letting it be no more than the means of covering the distance between two places on the map. Lord, recall my wandering mind to your presence: as a passenger I am never solitary.

WHETHER BY ROAD or rail or sea or air, I travel

in your company. I pray that you may accustom me to this truth, eliciting acts of prayer as the journey proceeds. Grant that if temptation or accident should threaten me on the way your grace may be with me. Mary, be with me now, in this journey, and at the hour of my death. Amen.

IN YOUR OWN LIFETIME, Lord, you endured a series of uprootings. At the Father's bidding you left Palestine for Egypt, Nazareth for Jerusalem, and then a whole sequence of changes. Always you welcomed the Father's will. I join myself with you in this, Lord, as in all else. I accept the Father's will that I should leave the place where I am and where I have been happy. I go gladly to do the work which he wants me to do somewhere else.

✠ WHEN LEAVING
A PLACE
WHICH WE LIKE

I HAVE ENJOYED being here, Lord, and I thank you for the time which I have spent in this place. Now that it is your will that I should move on, I come to you for the grace to do so in the right spirit. Grant me the gift of detachment. Grant me also the confidence which may make me face the future without dread. Whatever this wrench may be costing me emotionally, may I be spiritually able to meet the sacrifice.

THOUGH I SHRINK from partings I accept their necessity. I believe that they serve your purpose and that I cannot be the loser in yielding to them.

227

But let me in this particular instance have the grace to embrace, and not merely to endure, the change from one set of outward circumstances to another. In faith let me bow to these painful leave-takings as gladly as you bowed to the moment of your departure from the house of Mary and Joseph.

IN THEORY IT IS CLEAR to me that neither happiness nor holiness can be determined by geography, by where one happens to be. I know, Lord, that in whatever place I am I can be sure that your kingdom is within me, and that this is my true home.

✠ WHEN ARRIVING
AT A PLACE
WHICH WE DISLIKE

But in practice I find it hard either to expect happiness or to rise to the demands of holiness when I am living in surroundings which are uncongenial. Lord, give me more grace so that I may apply my knowledge to my present experience. Let the principle of your divine indwelling be my practical support.

IT WOULD BE FALSE to pretend that I rejoice in being where I am. But this gives me no right to indulge in resentment or wistful longings. While I am aware that there are other places where I would be happier than here, I am aware also that your divine providence has something for me here which I may not miss. Let me find here, in the setting which you have provided for me, the means towards the perfect fulfilment of your will. Happiness is subordinate to this. I must seek first the kingdom of God and all these things will be added.

I ACCEPT THE CIRCUMSTANCES which have resulted in my being where I am, and I accept the fact of not enjoying the result. I believe that here, of all the other places in the world, is where you want me to be. If this is so, it is the place best suited to my need. It is the one place on the globe from which, for the moment, you want me to worship you. Let me not waste this chance by sitting listless when I might be learning what it is you want me to do.

WHATEVER MY SENSE of not belonging and of homesickness, I have hope in you. *Et nunc quae est expectatio mea nonne Dominus?* You are my true setting, and I shall find no security in this life unless I look for it in union with you. When I can say *Dominus regit me et nihil mihi deerit,* I shall be free of this sad tendency to chafe at every change. Let me not put obstacles in the way of those graces which you are giving me here and now, and which are helping me—if only I will allow them—in the work of readjustment.

GRANT ME, LORD, the many graces which I shall need if I am to get the best out of this retreat. Let

✠ WHEN IN RETREAT

me see what it is that you want me to do; let me then have the strength to do it. I mean to open my soul to whatever it is that you have in store for me.

SHOW ME, LORD, how to get the best out of this retreat. Teach me what I ought to know. Draw me towards your Sacred Heart. Correct in me the many faults which I am either too lazy or too irresolute to attack myself.

GRANT THAT I MAY put no barriers between my soul and grace. During this retreat I pray especially that you may take undisputed possession of my soul, sweeping away my many excuses and evasions, and eliciting from me true acts of love.

EXPERIENCE HAS SHOWN me that it is not the beginning or the end of a retreat that is the difficulty, but the middle. Now that I have had time to get tired of it, and have not yet had time to benefit by its strength, may I be granted the grace of being faithful when I am bored.

IF MY RETREAT is teaching me wisdom, Lord, let it be the wisdom of the Spirit and not merely the wisdom of common sense. If I have to make decisions during this retreat, let me make them in the light of your love and not merely according to human prudence.

IF TRUE WISDOM is to know you, Lord, and not merely to know about you, I pray that your Spirit may draw me in this retreat to the true knowledge of yourself. Let me not waste time in speculation; bring me to the immediate exercise of love.

TEACH ME in this retreat, Lord, what you have been teaching the faithful since the Gospel was first preached. I know that the doctrine is the same for saints and sinners; what I need is to be told more forcibly what to do about it.

ALL I NEED is more of your Holy Spirit's influence in my soul. Given a greater awareness of your indwelling, I am bound to benefit by this retreat. May these few days of attention to the strictly interior working of grace have their lasting effect upon my life. Grant that more and more your will may operate in me, and that mine may give place to yours.

I KNOW THAT the graces of a retreat are not for the present only but also for the future. Grant I pray that the effects may go on when the time of retreat is over.

ON THIS THE CONCLUDING DAY of the retreat I pray particularly for perseverance. May the decisions arrived at, the resolutions made, the lights and inspirations received, be generously followed up when I go back to the routine of every day.

LET THE RECEIVING of thy body, O Lord Jesus Christ, which I, though unworthy, do presume to receive, not turn to me for judgment and condemnation, but according to thy mercy let it be profitable to me for the receiving of protection and healing both of soul and body.

✠ EUCHARISTIC PRAYERS

The Missal

ALMIGHTY AND EVERLASTING God, grant . . . that I may receive the bread of angels, the king of kings,

231

the lord of lords, with such reverence and humility, with such compunction and devotion, with such purity and faith, with such purpose and intention as may be profitable to my soul's salvation.

St. Thomas Aquinas

GRANT UNTO ME, I pray, the grace of receiving not only the sacrament of our Lord's body and blood, but also the grace and power of the sacrament. O most gracious God, grant me so to receive the body of thine only-begotten Son, our Lord Jesus Christ, which he took from the Virgin Mary, as to merit to be incorporated into his mystical body and to be numbered amongst his members.

St. Thomas Aquinas

I KNOW THAT I am not worthy to approach so great a mystery. But I know also that thou canst make me worthy, thou who alone canst make him clean who was conceived in sin, thou who makest of sinners men just and holy. By this almighty power of thine, I entreat thee, O my God, that thou wouldst grant to me, a sinner, the grace of celebrating this sacrificial mystery with fear and trembling, purity of heart and outpouring of tears, with spiritual gladness and heavenly joy. May my mind experience the sweetness of thy most blessed presence and enjoy the protection of thy holy angels about me.

St. Ambrose

I SEEK THY MERCY, O Lord, so that there may come down upon the bread to be sacrificed to thee the fullness of thy blessing and the sanctification of thy divinity. May there come down also, O Lord, the majesty of thy Holy Spirit even as of old it came down upon the sacrifices of the fathers.

St. Ambrose

GRANT ME, O God, so worthily to receive this most holy body and blood of thy Son that I may thereby receive forgiveness of all my sins, be filled with thy Holy Spirit, and find peace. For thou only art God and there is no other beside thee.

The Sarum Missal

I WILL TAKE THE BREAD of heaven, and will call upon the name of the Lord. Lord, I am not worthy that thou shouldst enter under my roof, but say only the word and my soul shall be healed. The body of our Lord Jesus Christ preserve my soul for everlasting life. Amen.

The Missal

WHAT RETURN SHALL I MAKE to the Lord for all that he has given me? I will take the chalice of salvation and call upon the name of the Lord. Praise be to the Lord. When I call upon his name I am safe from my enemies. The blood of our Lord Jesus Christ preserve my soul for everlasting life. Amen.

The Missal

THAT WHICH OUR MOUTHS have taken, Lord, may we possess in purity of mind; and may this present gift become for us an everlasting remedy.

The Missal

MAY THY BODY which I have taken, Lord, and the blood which I have drunk, cleave to every fiber of my being. Grant that no stain of sin may be left in me, now that I am renewed by this pure and holy sacrament.

The Missal

MAY THE TRIBUTE of my homage be pleasing to thee, Holy Trinity. Grant that the sacrifice which I, unworthy as I am, have offered in the presence of thy majesty may be acceptable to thee. Through thy mercy may it bring to me forgiveness as well as to all for whom I have offered it.

The Missal

SOUL OF CHRIST, make me holy. Body of Christ, be my salvation. Blood of Christ, take me out of myself. Water flowing from the side of Christ, wash me clean. Passion of Christ, give me strength. O kindest Jesus, hear my prayer. Hide me within my wounds. And let me never be parted from thee. Defend me from the villainous foe. Call me at the hour of death, and summon me into thy presence, there to praise thee with thy saints for ever. Amen.

St. Ignatius

HAVING BEEN ASKED by many to pray for them and for their intentions I come before you, Lord, and beg that you may attend to these requests. I pray as earnestly for those which I have forgotten as for those which I have remembered, as much for those which seemed trivial to

✝ REQUEST PRAYERS

me as for those which seemed to me important. I know that to the people making the requests there was urgency in the appeal, and this is what I hand on to you. See the need and the urgency, I pray you, Lord, and let neither my indifference nor unworthiness stand in the way of your grace.

IF I WERE TO MAKE a list of those people for whom I had at one time or another promised to pray, I would have to spend the whole of my prayer-time working my way down a column of names. Instead let me turn over the whole matter to you, confident that you will look after the needs of those who have requested a mention in my wretchedly inadequate prayers. Lord, your generosity is infinite: into this inexhaustible wealth of grace I drop my list. Grant that every intention there represented may appear before your divine mind as though no other petition were being put to you.

LORD, I HAVE BEEN ASKED to pray for many things: for fine weather, for rain; for success in this or that enterprise; for recovery from sickness and for the conversion from sin and error; for courage in the face of poverty, disgrace, loss of friends; for p e o p l e w h o a r e sad, lonely, old, tempted; for the souls of those who have died. Lord, I refer all these needs to you as though they were my own. Indeed, they *are* my own—made mine in the charity of your mystical body. And because they come from the mystical body they are yours also. Father, hear the prayer which comes from the faithful, from me, and from your Son.

As in the Old Law the priest of the week stood before you with the names of the twelve tribes inscribed upon a fillet which he wore upon his forehead, so I come before you with the requests of the faithful and the needs of the Church in my mind. Since you did not demand the explicit mention of each tribe in the priestly prayer, so I can assume that you do not require of me the explicit mention of every cause entrusted to my mediation. I present every intention which has been committed to me, Lord, in homage and trust before you. Graciously remember those whose needs I represent. And when you have heard these prayers, Lord, accept my grateful thanks. Amen.

What return shall I make to thee, O Lord, for all the good which I have received from thee? . . .

✝ PRAYERS OF SELF-GIVING

O Lord, I offer up to thee my body, my soul, all that I am, all that I shall do or suffer this day. Grant, O God, that all may tend to thy glory and to my salvation . . . I offer myself entirely to thee. Deign to make my heart like thine, meek and humble. Let me resemble thee in charity and kindness to all. Make me resigned to thy holy will, and grant that I may be worthy of that reward which thou hast promised to those who love thee faithfully here upon earth. Amen.

The Holy Trinity Book of Prayers

DIVINE HEART OF JESUS, I offer thee my poor actions to obtain the acknowledgment of every heart of thy sacred kingly power. In this way may the kingdom of thy peace be firmly established throughout all the earth. Amen.

The Raccolta

I VOW AND CONSECRATE to God all that is in me: my memory and my actions to God the Father; my understanding and my words to God the Son; my will and my thoughts to God the Holy Ghost. My heart, my body, my tongue, my senses and all my sorrows I consecrate to the sacred humanity of Jesus Christ who did not refuse to be betrayed into the hands of sinful men, and to suffer the torment of the cross.

St. Francis of Sales

IN ORDER THAT I MAY BE a living act of perfect love, I offer myself as a whole burnt offering to thy tender love, beseeching thee to consume me continually . . . with every heart beat I desire to renew this offering an infinite number of times until that day when the shadows shall vanish and I shall be able to re-tell my love in an eternal face-to-face with thee.

St. Theresa of Lisieux

DO THOU CONSUME in me all that can displease thee or resist thy holy will. Let thy pure love imprint thyself so deeply upon my heart that I shall never again be able to forget thee . . . in thee I desire to place all my happiness and all my glory, living and dying in bondage to thee.

St. Margaret Mary

TAKE ME; I give myself to thee. I entrust to thee all my actions; my mind that thou mayest enlighten it, my heart that thou mayest direct it, my will that thou mayest establish it, my misery that thou mayest relieve it, my soul and my body that thou mayest feed them. Eucharistic Heart of Jesus, whose blood is the life of my soul, may it be no longer I that live, but thou alone who livest in me.

The Raccolta

MY MOST LOVING JESUS, I consecrate myself today anew and without reserve to thy divine Heart. I consecrate my body with all its senses, my soul with all its faculties, and in short my entire being. I consecrate to thee all my thoughts, words, and deeds; all my sufferings and labors; all my hopes, consolations, and joys. And chiefly do I consecrate to thee this poor heart of mine to the end that it may love nothing save only thee, and may be consumed as a victim in the fire of thy love.

The Raccolta

MY LOVING JESUS, out of the grateful love I bear thee, and to make reparation for my unfaithfulness to grace, I give thee my heart, and I consecrate myself wholly to thee; and with thy help I purpose to sin no more.

The Raccolta

LORD, I OFFER MYSELF to you in union with your intention at the sacrifice of the Mass. I place myself with the host on the paten; I give myself with the wine in the chalice. Join me to your sacrificial prayer as it goes up from the altar in perfect praise to the Father. As you yielded yourself into the hands of men during the first Holy Week, so do I yield myself to whatever treatment I may receive from my fellow-men. As you entrust yourself to the care of human beings, your priests on earth, every time that Mass is offered, so do I entrust myself to the authority of your ministers in the Church. Lord, I am yours; do with me what you will.

LORD, MY PURPOSE is to deny you nothing. So far as I can say this and truly mean it, I surrender myself utterly and completely to your will. Have your way with me, ignoring my protests and efforts to escape. Whatever my superficial self may say by way of complaint, whatever the rebellion of my nerves and emotions, my will is that you should have the unqualified freedom of my being.

IF MY PRAYER, O God the giver of every good gift, assumes the form of a litany of petition, at least I need not feel that I am departing from Christian tradition. The Church's liturgy shows many such catalogues of requests. But since

✠ PRAYERS TO MEET COMMON CONTINGENCIES

we are urged by the early fathers, by St. Basil in

particular, to begin on a note of praise rather than petition, I address myself to you first in worship. *Laudamus te. Benedicimus te. Adoramus te. Glorificamus te. Gratias agimus tibi propter magnam gloriam tuam.* Lord, with every movement of my soul and with every cell of my body I pay homage to you. Blessed be your name.

In giving thanks for your great glory, I give thanks also for your great goodness to me. I am grateful, Lord, for every grace which you have ever given to me, to those dear to me, and to those whose needs I have mentioned in my prayers. I am grateful also for the mercy which you have shown to sinners, to the world at large, to the souls in purgatory. From the depths of my heart I am thankful, and will try to show my gratitude not only by returning thanks to you promptly in the future when you hear my prayers but also by readily accepting whatever sacrifices you may ask of me in the name of love.

Lord, let these following petitions be to your glory. Let also those petitions which I should be making but which, either because I have forgotten them or because I have been unaware of the need to make them, have fallen by the way, be heard and granted. Inspire me in my prayer that I may know what to ask for and how best to ask it. Teach me the secrets of prayer. Show me how I may please you always.

I pray for the Church. I pray for unbelievers

that they may come to a knowledge of the truth. I pray for the conversion of sinners. I pray for souls in purgatory. I pray for the tempted, the oppressed, the sick, the old and infirm, the lonely, the homeless, the poor, the embittered and those who in one way or another have made failures of their lives. Lord, come to the help of all these souls.

I PRAY ALSO for peace among nations. I pray that there may not be famines, failures in crops, plagues, earthquakes, or other natural scourges. Grant that if these things must come upon us for our sins, and certainly we deserve them, we may endure them in a spirit of penance. Grant an end to unemployment, social unrest, delinquency among the young, financial and political confusion. May men and women of every land come to learn the true values in life, discarding the false hopes of materialism and placing their security in you alone.

COMING CLOSER to myself, I pray for those who in any way depend upon me or to whom I owe obligations in justice or charity. May I never for one instant come between them and you, but on the contrary become a means of drawing them to their true happiness which is to be found only in yourself. May my family and my friends respond to your grace as completely as I myself want to respond; may they be rewarded as I myself hope, by your mercy, to be rewarded.

PRAYING NOW about my own personal needs, I ask that I may come increasingly to live in your light. May your will be increasingly fulfilled in me. Develop in me your own virtues, and grant that I may share in your prayer and sacrifice in such a way that I may take no credit for the work but on the contrary see in it the marvelous operation of your grace. Lead me through the avenues of love, humility, and self-sacrifice to the throne of the Father. My final perseverance is your gift, and I confidently ask for this. My merits are your wounds: I have no claim, no rights, no securities —beyond what you give to me from your own. You have given me yourself, so I have all. *In te, Domine, speravi; non confundar in aeternum.*